SCORE

Memoirs of A Weed Smuggler

By "Mika Airth" as told to Robert Loomis

Foreword: The 52-year Project

This book began in Fall 1969 at a friend's house. He had informed me he had a houseguest who had just returned from Mexico where he'd been on the verge of smuggling 680 kilograms of marijuana into the United States. The caper went sour when the Nixon administration popped Operation Intercept, the latest in the government's efforts to stem the tide of "dangerous drugs" into the United States from south of the border. Said my friend: "He arrived at my place, slept for 48 hours, then walked out of the bedroom and began reeling off stories that blew my mind. As a reporter, you should talk to this guy."

Intrigued, I arranged to meet the man who later called himself Mika Airth for purposes of our book venture. Our initial talk convinced me he had plenty of good material for a magazine piece. We started taping interviews.

My experience with marijuana up to then had been as a low-key user and occasional purchaser of a baggie of the weed, commonly called a "lid" in those days. I'd had my first hit on a joint offered by a friend at a party in 1961 and had over the ensuing years become a fairly regular weekend recreational and sometimes workday medicinal user to mellow out after deadline-ridden shifts at the newspaper where I worked, the Vallejo Times-Herald. In 1969, you could still buy a lid (one ounce) of good marijuana for $15 to $20, but the price went up after Operation Intercept. By then I considered the government's view of marijuana as a dangerous narcotic – a stance unchanged to this day at the Federal level, despite studies refuting its accuracy – a bad joke. So did a lot of others, especially those who participated in any way in the San Francisco Bay Area's so-called hippie scene. By 1969 marijuana was commonly seen at parties of all kinds, including some I attended at homes of "straight" friends.

Until interviewing Mika, I had never given much thought to what was involved in getting marijuana into the country. At the time, the majority of weed still came from south of the border, though Humboldt County's Emerald Triangle was beginning to take shape. Not much, if anything, had been written about the business of smuggling and dealing it. I had drifted along for some years in a pleasantly stoned state of ignorant bliss as to how the drug got into the United States. Mika opened my eyes.

On a professional level, it seemed the perfect opportunity to at last crack the nut of free-lance magazine journalism and end my frustrating and less than remunerative career as a newspaper reporter. I envisioned selling a piece to Esquire or Playboy and then having a successful magazine career (followed, of course, by best-selling books), all considerably more lucrative and rewarding than newspapers. By the time we had done two interview sessions, it was apparent that Mika had more than enough material for a book, not just an article. He was a charming and excellent story teller. I felt it would be comparatively easy to stitch together the interviews into the first nonfiction book about marijuana smuggling. We decided to go for it.

Mika then moved to San Francisco, where we continued our taping sessions. I would drive into the city from Vallejo after work and sit down with him in the living room of the house in the Upper Haight. After the first three sessions in Concord, we did twenty more sessions in San Francisco. Each session ranged from one to two and a half hours. Since we were partaking of Mika's excellent product during those sessions, the interview transcripts (which we paid Mika's brother's girlfriend to type up) had to be pieced together with literal cut-and-paste techniques using scissors, glue and the old newspaper copy paper on which they were typed. At one point I had chapters spread all over the floor of my study at home as I pieced the rough draft together. The age of computers was as yet still in the future, there was no easy, onscreen editing.

The result -- in early spring 1970 -- was a 460-page, double-spaced, very rough draft badly in need of further editing. We hoped it would be a good enough start to secure an advance from a publisher, after which Mika could retire to other business pursuits and I would have money to finance a new free-lance career. Because Grove Press had long been a bastion of underground and avant-garde publishing, I contacted them first through their West Coast editor in San Francisco, Donald M. Allen. Since deceased, Allen was known, among other things, as editor of The New American Poetry, 1945-1960. We visited him at his office and submitted the first draft to him, eager to hear his opinion. He liked it. We then said we wanted "a big advance." How much would that be, he asked. We suggested $10,000, which in those days seemed like a lot of money. Allen said that shouldn't be a problem if Grove's people back east liked it as much as he did.

He sent the manuscript to Grove in New York City. Mika and I anxiously waited for the contract and big check, and agreed on a 60-40 split beyond the advance. We also consulted San Francisco attorney Rommel Bondoc (also now deceased) to try to find out what our options might be for shielding Mika's identity when Grove offered us a contract. We were extremely paranoid about that. We feared the manuscript might fall into the wrong hands, and that the government might come after us after publication because of the nature of the book. We were so worried that we destroyed the interview cassette tapes as soon as they were transcribed (which I regret deeply now). Bondoc assured us a properly protective contract was possible and advised us to let him see any contract before signing. We left his office with visions of literary and other fame dancing in our heads. Mika wanted the contract to stipulate that he would audition to play himself if the book became a movie. Given his charm, I thought it entirely possible he might get the role.

Then came ... nothing. No word, no contract, nothing. I was unable for more than two years after the book went east to determine any specifics about what transpired. Neither Donald M. Allen nor we could get any definitive word from Grove's people back east on the manuscript. Allen finally gave me a phone number in New York. "I can't get anything out of them, maybe you can," he said.

I made numerous calls. Each time I talked to someone different. Finally, one afternoon I reached someone who told me. "I think the book was sent back to readers for re-evaluation. My guess is that it got sent home with a reader. I'll try to track it down for you." My hopes rose a bit then, though the part about a re-evaluation didn't seem good. I had expected that with Allen's support, the book would sail right through to publication. Again, for some weeks I heard nothing further. Again I called. The same person answered and told me she had been unable to trace the manuscript but "a lot of people have been fired here. I'm pretty sure it got sent home with one of our readers who got fired and never was returned. I'll try again, but don't be surprised if you don't hear from me and I'm not here anymore when you call again."

By then, I'd pretty much given up hope. Mika had moved on to other endeavors and we were not in close contact. In those days, there were no Internet or cell phones to ease communication. By 1972, I had taken a new job with the Oakland Tribune. I sent a somewhat further edited manuscript to several other publishers but got no nibbles. It was not until 1974 that the first book about smuggling was published, Jerry Kamstra's "Weed – Adventures of A Dope Smuggler." Where ours was more adventure story than how-to, Kamstra's focused more on the nuts and bolts of smuggling. Its publication pretty much laid to rest any remaining hope I had for publication, even though I felt ours was by far more entertaining. I still feel that way. But I had jeopardized my marriage and shirked my parenting duties while working so many hours on "Score" while holding a full-time job. I felt it was time to move on.

Sometime later I stumbled across an article in a trade journal at De Lauer's News Stand in Oakland that provided the final piece in the Grove Press manuscript puzzle. It reported more than 200 people had been fired at Grove Press after an attempt to unionize the publisher failed. Those who voted to go union had been fired, among them almost certainly the reader who had the original manuscript.

After that, I saw Mika only on widely-separated occasions over the next 30 or 40 years. At one point he lived in Hawaii and ran a charter boat business. I knew he loved boats, so it fit. He and his wife "Tanya" had reconciled long since. Later I heard they had bought a house in the Northwest and were happily living there. We all grew older. Mika's brother ("Samuel" in our book) died at age 65 in 2007. Mika died at age 69 in 2010. I had been busy just living my own workaday life. My energy outside journalism had gone more and more into music and less and less into writing. I still regret not staying in closer touch with them. I also feel some guilt at not having pursued "Score" with more diligence way back when. As they say, life is what happens while you are making other plans.

So much has changed since the initial draft of this book was written. Thirty-seven states have now moved to legalize at least medicinal pot. Seven states and the District of Columbia have decriminalized and legalized recreational use at. At this writing, the Federal government still refuses to budge on its view of marijuana as a Schedule 1 dangerous narcotic, all studies and information to the contrary notwithstanding.

Mika's story is as entertaining as ever, and sheds light on the history of marijuana in the United States before the Emerald Triangle and the trend to legalize pot. Rest in peace, Mika and Samuel, thanks for the great times and great stories.

Enjoy!

Appreciations

Most of all, to Beverly, Devin and Shannon Loomis for living through the family time I lost while working on the book. To Beverly, especially, for acting as a second, efficient set of eyes in editing this version. My love to you all.

To C., who worked so hard transcribing those cassette tapes. To Tom for introducing me to Mika Airth. To Mika's wife "Tanya" for meeting with me to discuss the book 47 years after its inception. To the late Donald M. Allen for his efforts on our behalf. To those who tried to point me in the right direction with the at last edited version. Lastly, to the nation's mainstream media and voters for finally waking up to the fact that marijuana is not the killer narcotic so long depicted by government officials who have their own agendas for keeping it illegal. Better late than never, I suppose. Time will tell. If nothing else, it will thin our swollen prison population.

And of course, to Mika, who shared his stories.

Robert Loomis
October 2017

Chapter One
1970: The Dark Side of Mexico

It wasn't until the other night, the first night I could really relax in about six months, that I realized what I'd been through down there this year, all the hassles and all they involved. While I was there I didn't think about it too much, I just did whatever needed doing, step by step. But the other night I got loaded and relaxed and it suddenly flashed on me all I'd been through and it just BLEW my mind! Just "Waaaagh! What's been going on? Did I do all that? This is impossible!"

See, I was originally supposed to be in Mexico for a month, but it turned into five or six months with nothing to show for it! I lost my close relationships: my wife, a couple of friends, my brother — and a whole lot of bread for which people were waiting, dig? And I lost my peace of mind. I thought when I got back here I was going to have syphilis, elephantiasis, malaria and yellow fever. It seemed like all that just had to follow after everything else that went wrong. And everybody involved was so torn up, man, physically, mentally and spiritually. Just ... twisted. I got to the point where I was actually ready to start killing people. I carried a gun around a long time before I reached that point, and it was just to scare people away, because I figured if I carried the big gun people would be less likely to fuck with me than if I was somebody who had lots of money but no gun. But I finally actually got to the point where I was ready to use that gun. That was a different kind of mind set completely. See, if someone threatens you with a gun then you get to the point where if you're carrying one, then next time, up those bastards, man, I'll drill 'em!

There's this really dark side of Mexico. Mexico is like this facade and once you get beyond that facade into the black heart of it ... I mean, it's like pulling-a-snake-apart-with-your-bare-hands death. Like that iguana. Domingo, my connection, the guy who's with my ex now, Domingo killed an iguana on the front porch one night after playing with it for a while. He tied its legs behind it and kicked it around for a while, then put his foot on its neck and grabbed its tail and pulled until he broke its neck. And just left it there bleeding on the porch. "*Muuuuy muerto,* heh-heh-heh." Very dead. And yet these gentle, loving things can happen the next minute.

See, if you're talking to a Mexican, it's a Spanish Indian that's involved in the business-establishment, government trip. It's got nothing to do with bloodlines except in the sense that the trip is held together by a mixture of Spanish and Indian. That's probably what Mexican really is. The Indians, a lot of them have the Mexican thing happen, a lot don't. Anyway, there's this black side throughout Mexico, maybe it originated with the Spanish, they were a pretty bloodthirsty bunch of cats for a long time. Whatever it is, it's there, this black side. Life and death mean nothing. These cats have gone beyond despair. They've come so close to dying so many ways and so many times by the time they're 30 years old that they figure it could happen at any moment and they just step right out of it. They don't build houses until they're 35 or 40 years old and they figure they're only going to live till they're 50 or 55, so they build houses that might fall down a couple of times between now and when they die. When one gives way, build another one. Sticks and straw. Yet I met some groovy people, Indians mostly. But still, man, it's so ... it's like a coiled snake. Walking a tightrope, those people.

I mean death happens all around you., all the time there. People get killed violently, instantaneously, in all kinds of ways. Like the heat rolls up and goes into a bar and gets two guys and drags 'em outside and shoots 'em. Or a whole family disappears. Or the coconut growers revolt against the government and they have a shootout. That happened about three years ago in front of the Growers Hall or some governmental agency or something, they had a shootout between two factions and something like twenty-eight people were killed and sixty-six were wounded, including sixteen innocent bystanders or something like that. And this was in Acapulco within a few years ago.

Last year while we were down there I think during November or December there was a mountain bandit who went on a rampage and in about two weeks killed the mayors of eleven towns in the state of Guerrero. Somebody had squealed on one of his gang and they'd slapped the guy in jail, so after the boss man busted the cat out he went looking for the snitch. He found out it was a mayor of some town but not which one, so he put out word that he was going to kill a mayor a day till he got the one he wanted. So he began killing. It was eleven or thirteen or something like that that he killed before he finally grabbed one guy he thought knew who the snitch was and tortured him until he told who it was. Then he turned that guy loose and killed the squealer and disappeared back into the hills. And nobody's heard or seen anything of him since.

That kind of shit happens all the time in Mexico. The black side of Mexico. So going down there to score weed is *not* a joke, man. You talk to anybody who's ever done it and they'll tell you about some incredible hassles. When you're moving around bunches of weed, you're moving some bulk and you don't always know who you're dealing with. But you may not realize all that till you've gone down there and gotten in the middle of it.

So after this last trip it didn't hit me what I'd been through until that night I sat down and got stoned and thought about it. Then, "Whoa!" As I think back on it, I see how things have brought me to where I want to be out of the smuggling business for good.

Chapter Two
1964: Just A Straight Kid

Okay, how I got into this underground trip and into weed smuggling. When I first came to San Francisco I was really a straight kid. I mean I was living with Tanya, and we weren't married, but I intended to marry her as soon as I got a divorce. I had a wife and a couple of kids back home, but other than that, I mean I didn't smoke weed, I'd seen it a couple of times but I wasn't interested in it. I didn't even know anybody who did smoke it. When we got to San Francisco we didn't have any money so we thought we'd go to the San Francisco Art Institute because art institutes in about every city in the world have students looking to share apartments. So we went there and saw these people's names, Bill and Mary Smith call them. We didn't have jobs but we intended to get work, so we go over to the place. Mary was there and invited us in. We told her what our scene was, that Tanya was under 18 and that her parents were still chasing us around, that we didn't have any money but we were going to get jobs. She invited us to stay for dinner. She said Bill would be home soon and we could talk to him and that as far as she was concerned, we could stay there. We had dinner with them and he said sure, move in and pay us when you get it together.

Maybe a week after that we got jobs, but we were walking to work every day, we didn't have money for bus fare and at that point they were buying us food. Bill was in the habit of getting up late because he wasn't working, he was working on a book, so he usually got up around 10 or 11 o'clock and by that time we were long gone to work. But he got up early one morning and noticed me talking with Tanya about calculating the amount of time it took me to walk to work because I'd been missing it a bit and needed to leave earlier. He realized that we really didn't have *any* money and when I came back from work that night there was a check from him for $125 on the table in our room with a note saying "Here's some spending money until you get your first paycheck. Pay me back whenever it's convenient." I mean the cat was a mind-blower!

It turned out he smoked weed.

He kept it from us for a long time, for the first four or five months we lived there. We didn't even know he used it. Then one day he mentioned it to me and I told him I wasn't uptight about it so he started smoking around me. Eventually I started smoking a little now and then. I mean I was really a straight cat otherwise, like I was working in this department store as a clerk, you know, gray flannel suit, rep-stripe tie, wingtips, short haircut. I got up at 8 o'clock in the morning, I was at work at 8:30 and worked until 5:30 and until 9 on Friday nights. I mean I was a really straight-shootin' cat, right?

Then I got my draft notice.

Well, that was a whole different trip. That changed a lot of things. That really makes you decide. It's like they're asking, "Are you with us or against us?" Well, it didn't take but about 10 seconds to make up my mind which side of that I was on, because I mean, you know, it was nothing but cowardice! (laughs)

No, my reaction was "Look, what you people are having all these fights about is none of my business. If somebody attacks me personally or my old lady or somebody in my family, that's self-defense, I can understand that. But for me to be living in San Francisco on Telegraph Hill and playing tennis in the sun and sailing in Sausalito then all of a sudden get a letter that says 'We want you to come fight for us because we're too old.' My immediate reaction was, 'If you say it's worth dyin' for, you go die for it and then I'll believe you.'"

So I told Bill about getting my notice and he says, "Oh, yeah? And you don't want to go? Don't worry about it, you won't have to go. I'll come up with something, don't worry about it."

Turns out he had gotten out of the draft, too.

Bill's father was a government official. When he was living at home he rode to high school in a chauffeured limousine. When I was living with Bill his father sent him a picture of himself that he'd had taken, very dapper looking, small-boned little man with a very trim, neat mustache, holding a pipe, looking like he is smoking a pipe, but he really doesn't smoke a pipe it's just to create the illusion of an Oxford, contemplative statesman sort of cat. So Bill promptly glued this picture to the lid of the john so that when the seat was up it formed a frame.

Bill had lived in Europe for a long time and had hitchhiked back and forth through the Berlin sector taking weed into West Berlin from West Germany, which was really sort of a brave stunt. When he got his induction notice he was living the good life in Paris and wasn't about to go. He locked himself in a closet, a very small, cramped closet with a bare lightbulb, and sat down on the floor and stared at one spot on the floor until he could make his eyes tear and the tears were running off his face. He had people come by intermittently and suddenly pound on the door. And he took a bunch of stimulants to keep himself awake and get his nerves all jangled. He stayed in there four days!

On the evening of the fifth day he went to the local induction center on some Army base near Paris. There are like 25 guys, and they call 25 names and 24 guys answer. So pretty soon they figure the 25th guy is the one sitting there not saying anything, just sitting in the corner crying. He's just sitting there staring at the floor, man, with tears running down his face, looking like a crazy motherfucker. So they ask him his name and he doesn't answer, he just sits there crying. They ask him to come with them and he doesn't say anything, doesn't look up, just stares and cries. And pretty soon these officers are all standing over him talking about him saying things like "Oh, we got a case on

15

our hands here. He's shrink meat for sure!"

Finally somehow he lets them take him to the psychiatrist and he just completely blows the psychiatrist out. He gives inane answers to the questions. The psychiatrist finally gets tired of playing games and decides either he's really crazy or else he wants out bad enough to play this game, which also means he's crazy and they don't want him.

So Bill keeps telling me "Don't worry about it, I'll get you out."

I come home from work one Friday night and on Monday at 6:30 in the morning I'm going for my physical. Bill says, "Okay, take a hot bath."

"You're sure this is gonna work?" I say. "What're you gonna do?"

"Never you mind," he says. "Part of the way it will work is that you have to be surprised at various stages, so just do what I tell you and you'll get out."

So I take a hot bath. I get out of the bath and he has my old lady manicure my fingernails and toenails and put a couple of coats of clear polish on them. And from then on, the whole weekend was No-Doz, coffee, dexedrine, hot baths and people keeping me awake and him doing things like taking my skivvies and T-shirts down to the laundromat and washing them with a red sweatshirt so they come out a nice, brilliant pink. Then manicuring my toenails and fingernails again and buying me some pants that are one size too small. By this time I'm so absorbed in what he's going to do that like "I put my life in your hands, okay, go!"

So on Monday I'm supposed to report at 6 in the morning and about 4:30 in the morning he starts to get dressed. I ask where he's going and he says, "I'm going with you."

"I don't think they'll let you do that," I say, and he says, "Oh, yes they will."

I put on all the clothes. He's got a pair of brand-new, scrubbed white tennies for me, white socks, a pair of suntans with a razor-edge crease and some kind of funky-looking wool T-shirt. He puts on a pair of black pants, boots with high heels, and a ruffled blouse and throws one of his wife's sweaters over his shoulders. Puts mascara on his eyelashes and a little lipstick on, and takes a whole 8-ounce bottle of White Shoulders perfume and dumps it over his head. Then hands me a bottle of Aphrodisia to do the same. Man, people on the bus going downtown moved away from us!

We get to the downtown office where we're supposed to check in and take a bus over to the induction center in Oakland and I go to check in and I think well, this is the point where he's really not going to be able to make it, they'll check everybody on the bus and he won't be let on. But I know what's going on now so I figure I'll be able to carry on by myself without Bill. I mean, I'm ready to do anything, I'm ready to stand in the middle of the examination room and piss down my leg, I don't care, man. I figure any pain I can endure that day is better than the potential pain for two or three years and my possible early demise. So I check in and go out to get on the bus and Bill's already on the bus! "I just walked on," he says.

So everybody gets on the bus and it's full and one guy is standing in the aisle. The driver gets on. He's supposed to have exactly one busload of people, no more and no less, and he says, "All right, there's somebody on this bus that's not supposed to be here! I'm going to call off the names, everybody respond!"

He starts to call off the names and he calls mine and I answer and a few names later he calls another name and Bill answers. And the other guy doesn't say anything! And I know the other guy's on the bus, so there is still one too many people. So what's the driver going to do, check everybody's I.D.? He finally just decides fuck it, let the

Army hash it out after we get to Oakland. He's just a private, chartered bus driver, it's not his hassle. He's paid to drive, not keep track of who's who.

We get to the induction center in Oakland and go to a room where everyone has to fill out their papers. They hand us a bunch of blank forms and we all sit down at little desks, everybody but Bill, who's standing looking over my shoulder. There's a soldier who's a monitor who tells us to fill out the forms in pencil only and so on and Bill pulls out a lettering pen used for calligraphy and tells me, "Letter it, in ink." Okay, I'm sitting there making all these beautiful letters and Bill's standing over my shoulder telling me how to answer the questions and the monitor finally wakes up and wonders what's going on. He comes over and looks down at me and my form and says "What the hell are you doing?" I say I'm filling out the form. He says "Can't you read? It says right at the top 'Use pencil only on this form.'" I say "I never use pencil. You can't make good letters with a pencil. It's not possible. You can't get the lifts." He says "What? Are you kidding? I don't care about any of that. You have to use a pencil!"

So I very reluctantly put down the pen and pick up the pencil and the monitor turns to Bill and says "What're you doing here?" Bill says "I came in with Mika. He has a *terrible* time with paperwork and I came along to help him."

And the cat says "Hey! You'll have to wait in the waiting room!"

So they usher Bill out. He tries to come back in a couple more times while we fill out paperwork but he never gets through the door before the monitor says "Back in the waiting room!"

So on the form I leave blank things like whether I ever had the mumps, whether I was homosexual, whether I was a drug addict. When we get up to get in line and go somewhere else there's a guy checking our papers and he says "You've missed a question here ... and a couple on this page ... you have to answer all these questions." I said, "I'm sorry but it's really impossible for me to answer those." He looks at me and says "What about this: you ever had mumps? Now you must know whether you had mumps or not."

I say "No, I don't know if I ever had mumps. I think I did, but I'm not sure."

He says "Well, just put in 'yes.' "

I say "Oh, I can't do that because if I say I've had mumps and I haven't I could get in a lot of trouble."

He tells me no, no, don't worry about it just say yes, and I say "Look! Right at the bottom it says a ten-thousand dollar fine and/or 10 years in prison for falsifying evidence on this form. It doesn't allow you to say maybe or I don't know, so I really can't say yes or no."

He says "You have to answer every question on the form, those are the regulations."

"Look," I say, "I'm not in the Army yet. And, uh, ten thousand dollars and/or 10 years in prison? I can't answer it!"

He says, "Okay you, in there," and steers me off to a room on the side. Pretty soon another guy comes in and we go through the same trip about the form and finally he just marks the answers what he thinks they are. By that time he figures I probably have had the mumps, I probably am homosexual and I'm probably a dope addict besides. So he just marks yes, yes, yes. I say "I won't sign that." He says, "You probably won't have to." And I think, oh, good, things are going our way.

So next everybody strips down to their shorts to get weighed and give urine samples. Everybody else strips down to their white jockey shorts and I strip down to my pink jockey shorts. Right away I start getting funny looks. I go to sit down on one of the benches, each holding maybe ten guys. Only one bench had room to sit. There were two guys on that bench and when I go over and sit down, they stand up! I can hear guys behind me saying shit like "Look at that faggot, doesn't that make y' sick?" And I'm thinking, "That's all right motherfucker, you're going, I ain't."

So about the time I start to go in to give my urine sample, Bill tries to run in again and they throw him out. I give my urine sample and then they take the blood sample. Of course I pass out. I'm sitting there in the chair with my elbow on the desk and they put the needle in my arm and I look at the blood and just go "Ahhhh! Ooooh!" and fall over on the floor. They go for it, they come over and pick me up, put me on a bench, put a cold compress on my head and tell me to take it easy for a few minutes. After that, we go in where a guy says, "Awwright! Everybody bend over and touch your toes." And everybody in the room bends over and comes as close as possible to touching their toes. I bend about two inches and stop. And the guy comes over and asks what's the matter. I tell him I can't bend any further, I had a back injury, which I did, I broke my back once. He tells me to bend over till it hurts and I bend another inch and say, "It's unbearable! Ooooo! It Hurts! No further!" He tells me to stand up and then here comes Bill again: "Mika, are you all right?" I wave and say "Yes, Billy, I'm all right, everything's fine."

About this time the chief medical officer comes in and grabs Bill by the back of his shirt and pulls him out of the room. About five minutes later he comes back and asks "Is there a Mika Airth in here?" I daintily raise my hand and he says. "You! Come with me!" It's psychiatrist time. I go in and sit in front of the psychiatrist and he says, "Well, now, here you have marked the form that, um, you have homosexual inclinations."

I tell him no, I didn't mark that yes, the guy in the other room did it and I wouldn't sign it. He says "Well, do you in fact feel that you have homosexual inclinations or

20

tendencies?" I say, "Define what you mean by 'homosexual inclination.' " And he says "You know what I mean." And I say, "No, no I don't." So he says "Do you prefer men to women?"

I say, "Oh, my! That's impossible for me to answer. Some of my friends are men and some are women."

"Well, have you ever had sex with a man?"

"What constitutes having sex with a man?"

I make him define everything exactly and then I say, "Well, yes, I guess so." And he scribbles something on the form. Then he says, "Now here's a question about drugs. Have you ever been addicted to any habit-forming drugs, narcotics or barbiturates? You marked that yes."

I tell him no, I didn't mark that yes, that guy in the other room did. "Well, have you been?"

"Well," I say, "I just sort of take anything I can whenever I can get it, y'know? Somebody comes along with some heroin, yeah, okay." Which was bullshit, I'd never take heroin, I have better sense than that. Get strung out on fucking smack or speed, man, it really just ruins you. If I have to stay up I'll take some bennies to do it, but in a couple of days I start to hurt. It deteriorates your body in a hurry. So he scribbles something else on the form and says, "Okay, you can go out, you can get dressed." I get dressed and he says, "Go wait in the waiting room." They're calling names and people are going up to a desk and being given a slip of paper, and when they call my name I go up, and Bill walks up with me, and the guy says in a very formal tone, "You've been found unfit for military service under current standards." And then he turns to Bill and says, "Okay, you can take him home now. Take good care of him."

And we go over to Mike's Pool Hall and get drunk.

So that's what really got me into the underground. I had never done anything like that before, but once I'd decided … that trip did it, finished me with the establishment.

Chapter Three
1964-1967: Early Days — The Haight And Beyond

  So that's pretty much when I began getting into the art community and the people who were into weed and draft resistance and the peace movement, that whole trip. I don't remember what year it was, a long time ago, ancient history. But I kept my job for months after that. After the first one I worked another straight job for a while, but I was gradually getting more and more out of it. Pretty soon I started going to the art institute, and began building up a freelance photography business. Then I quit my regular job. What made me quit was my first acid trip. I went down to Big Sur on a Saturday and took LSD and on Monday morning I called work and said "Forget it, I got better things to do with my time." And I started dealing.

  I actually got into it by accident. I knew a guy who was a painter. I was a photographer and we had a couple of the same classes at the art institute, so I would go over to his house and get stoned. He had a friend who was a distributor for the first Owsley acid who was just giving him hits and then he was putting himself through art school by selling it. At the time, it was still legal. Friends of mine had started asking me about acid when they found out I'd taken it, and since I could get it, I would get it and give it to them, or sell it for forty cents a hit. I could get 200 hits for that price. At first I was just giving it away, then I thought, "Hey, this cat I'm getting it from is putting himself through art school, so the hell with it, maybe I should just ..." And the people who were buying it were buying in quantities big enough that you knew they were selling and making a profit. So I decided to turn a little profit myself.

  When I hooked up with this guy the artist was getting his acid from, he was also doing kilos of weed, so I started dealing kilos. The first kilo I bought was on the basis that I had $35 and two other friends had $35 each and that was enough to buy one kilo. So we did that and then I realized I could turn 'em over and make money, so I started doing that. Then it just started building.

By that time I was living on Ashbury Street and it was the beginning of the Haight-Ashbury, the beginnings of the Flower Children and all that. So that's how I got started, dealing lids on Haight Street. Me and Superspade and Spade Johnny and Shob Carter and Flyin' Eddie and Goldfinger, cats like that, outasight sorta cats, man!

The cops killed Superspade. I mean, it never came out officially that they killed him, but that's what I think happened. I'm certain of it. Because he hated them and they hated him. He rode around on a motorcycle, did all his dealing from the bike because he figured if they ever tried to catch him, he could get away with his stash and get rid of it and be gone before they could catch him. He was a very smart cat. Everybody that heard about Superspade thought he was just a black motorcycle cat, but he had been educated at Dartmouth or somewhere like that, he was a really intelligent cat. And he just hated the heat, just hated 'em. He was into dealing acid and weed mainly, just psychedelics, no heroin, maybe occasional speed but for the most part it was all hash and grass and acid. He got hip pretty quick to all the plainclothesmen who were working around the Haight-Ashbury. He'd see 'em standing somewhere with their cameras under their coats checking out somebody's house and he'd swing by on his bike and lace the curb with a couple of cherry bombs. Those bombs'd go off and these cats would whip around and fling their coats open and pull out their pistols and just blow their whole act. Or he'd ride up beside an unmarked car and say, "Evening, copper, what's happenin'? Think I'll ride with y' for a while and point y' out to my friends." Shit like that. So they hated him. His body was found out at the beach in a sleeping bag, shot in the back of the head. Tell me the cops didn't do it. Maybe not, but that's what I think.

And Shob Carter got killed, got his arm cut off. That made the newspapers. The scene was, I had been doing some business with Shob, he was a very groovy cat, played the flute, a good flute player; and he made it dealing grass. Didn't deal anything else, didn't deal acid or anything like that. At one point he lived with me, I had a place at the corner of Haight and Ashbury, had a big marijuana flag sticking out the window. One of the cats living there was doing rock concerts at one of the rock halls here in town, so I had all the people doing his artwork and poster distribution and the managers from the bands and some of the cats from the bands that this promoter was friends with coming in and out and scoring weed.

There was another cat in another room who was doing a border thing and had all his people coming in. He was dealing from right there out of the crib. He'd roll in with kilos of weed in boxes in the back seat of his car and he'd put 'em in his bedroom and jack his phone into the wall and lay down on his bed and fire up a joint and and start calling people. And he'd lay there dealing weed until it was all gone. And I'm living there in another room and at one point Shob Carter was living there. He had his old lady and his room and he did all his dealing away from the house, he never brought any of his people to the house, he never kept his stash in the house, I mean, he was cool.

Then I got back from one of my Mexico trips where I was gone several months because things fell apart, and Shob had moved out to the avenues in the Sunset District. I moved to Marin County but I began doing business with him. If I brought in a hundred kilos, I'd front him fifty, just take 'em to his house, drop 'em off and he'd take 'em to his stash and deal 'em off and bring me the bread. He was trustworthy, I mean, like that fifty kilos would cost something like $5,000 to $7,000 that he would owe me and he would always pay me within a few days. It was never longer than a week. Always righteously honest, always

24

very cool.

But apparently not cool enough.

Because among the people who knew he was dealing and thus probably had some cash was a cat who was just, unpredictably probably, just a screwball, a total nutcase. And the guy came over to Shob's on the pretext of scoring some weed and tried to rip off Shob. They got into it and he ends up killing Shob. But dig this: he cuts off one of Shob's arms and wraps it in a paper bag, takes Shob's car keys, puts the arm in the back seat of Shob's car and drives up the coast! I mean …

We drove by about four hours after they found the body. I started driving up the street and there were cop cars, man, there must have been seven cop cars with their lights flashing. There was an ambulance there and they were just taking him away. And we go "Wow! Fuck! What's going on?" The cat who was with me says he's going to go find out and I say "Man, I'll tell you what: you can go find out if you want to but if I'm going to do any finding out it's going to be from a distance. Because there's police there and if you go start asking questions and if it's Shob's place this scene is happening in, then they're going to nail your ass to a fuckin' tree and find out what's happening with *you*." So we're sort of sitting there wondering what to do when here comes this chick who had been Shob's old lady until a couple of months before that. They had split up but she had just come by to see him. She told us that not only was Shob dead, but one of his arms was missing. They found the guy who did it three, four days later someplace up the Mendocino coast just driving down the road with the fucking arm still in the back seat of the car.

That was right about when things started to get real heavy around the Haight. That's when everybody started moving out. Pretty soon all the dealers were living in Marin County, wouldn't go near the Haight-Ashbury. It really changed. Like in the beginning there were never any street people. We used to go down in the afternoons, hang around down on Haight Street, but I mean everybody had a crib, everybody was taking care of their own scene, had something going that was making bread — they were dealing or they had a clothing store or they'd been working for a while and saved up enough money not to work for a while or they were freelance photographers or artists who were making enough or they were going to school — everybody had some kind of trip. It was an art community, really. It was just really groovy.

Then it started getting a lot of press and a lot of people moving in from all over the country, 15-year-old runaways whose parents would get uptight when they found out their kids were in the Haight-Ashbury. So the cops were running around looking for runaways all the time and using that as an excuse to search people. And people started getting uptight and throwing rocks at the cops. Plus, when it became obvious to the whole world that there was a big dope-dealing, underground, black market kind of scene it attracted all the vultures who always flock around that, the rip-off artists. They started to roll into town by the dozens. Anybody who had any sense moved out pretty quick.

See, it used to be that I'd be holding twenty or thirty thousand dollars waiting for some acid deal to come down and people would just show up at the door and we'd smoke a joint and a guy would throw five-thousand dollars on the table and take his dope and walk out and say "I'll see you in a couple of days." And the deal would go down and cats would come around and pick it up and that was all there was to it. Then the ripoffs began. You fronted somebody some money and "Pssssh!" they just disappeared. Never see 'em again. I ended up having to pay back twenty-four, twenty-five thousand dollars that got ripped off one way or another. I'd have some kilos stashed in a warehouse and somebody would buy kilos from somebody else and then track 'em around till they figured out where the stash was and they'd rip it off. Stuff like that.

That's when everybody got paranoid and started getting big dogs. A big dog will slow down a cat with a pistol because he'll know he can plug you or the dog but not both. And whichever's left will be on his ass. A big dog will keep people from nosing around. A dog'll even keep the cops from beating guys up. And cops love to beat people up. But they'd have a hard time explaining a lot of dead dogs. Plus the dogs give you a chance to flush the toilet once or twice if you've only got a little taste around.

Anyway, the Haight scene and the underground scene got really far out, really heavy. The level of resistance rose. Like the Black Panthers are getting ready to try to defend themselves if they possibly can because it's obvious that the heat are trying to wipe 'em out. When they start killing people in their beds, like Chicago, that's genocide, right? When the white pigs break into somebody's crib and kill 'em in their sleep in their beds, that's genocide. So the Panthers know what's going on.

So the cops are harassing everybody — and for what, weed? They're not uptight about the weed itself, they're uptight because they know that if people sit around getting stoned and talking about things instead of watching TV, pretty soon they add two plus two and get three often enough that they start figuring out what's happening with the establishment, and they don't want that. But now they've got a real underground on their hands. So they're freaking out, and harassing even people who are on their side. A friend of mine got busted for shoplifting after he bought a toy for his kid and got his sales receipt and tried to walk out of the store with his toy. It was too large for a bag, so he thought he'd just carry it out. They stopped him and ended up arresting him, took him downtown, and by the time they ran him around at 880 Bryant Street (a police holding facility in San Francisco), he'd had it! He's an honest man, employed, carrying bucks, and the receipt but they treated him like dirt. He used to put down the hippies, the peace marchers, the draft resisters, but now he's got to look at all that from a new viewpoint.

What they don't realize, these establishment cats, is that there's a lot of straight people into weed now. I smoked weed in New York with the wife of a U.S. senator. They busted a Maryland senator for coming into the country with sixteen or seventeen pounds of weed! I had a friend who was working on one of the big political campaigns, advising them on how to appeal to young people on the left, and he was also scoring for 'em! Jump in a jet in San Francisco and fly to D.C. with five kilos of really boss weed for campaign headquarters!

They can't possibly beat it because the people who are involved are the sons and daughters of powerful people. The movement is, by and large, very well educated. They'll be running the country soon. And everybody with a lick of sense knows that eventually weed is going to have to be legalized. Otherwise it's just Prohibition all over again. You'd think they'd learn that anytime you start busting people for doing something they dig doing, it makes a lot of others wonder why they dig it so much. And pretty soon everybody wants to try it. I go home to visit my mother and she says "Okay, you're living in San Francisco, where's the marijuana? I want to try it." And my mother's no radical!

So except for the fact that they're screwing up a lot of people's lives behind court and what it costs them for attorneys and bail and harassment and jail and worry and all that, it's sort of funny. Because it's like watching some cat walking down the street beating himself on the head with a club.

But anyway, when Shob got killed that was when the Haight started changing. When the scene first started to happen there was only one hip store on Haight Street, the Grateful Dead was still using their old name, I think, the

Warlocks, and they lived just down the street from us. There were some hip people around but it was groovy. We'd have a Sunday afternoon party, people'd come over, get stoned, get a little drunk, dance, have some popcorn. Everybody had a good time, nothing heavy, no big crowds, no big scene happening, it was just a small community. You'd walk down the street, people'd be standing around smiling those illegal smiles.

But it started getting bigger and bigger. We started out standing on Haight selling lids and then suddenly we were making movements across the border with hundreds of kilos.

And the way I got into smuggling from south of the border was, this buddy of mine, Benny, knew some people in L.A. that we met through a friend. This friend had a setup that enabled him to fly around with lots of kilos of weed and never get busted. So he'd fly to L.A. and pick up kilos and bring 'em up to San Francisco. Then Benny and I would sell it and split the bread. The cat who was selling it down there got into a bigger business, increased what he could get across the border to where he could bring in up to a couple hundred kilos a week. But he didn't have the time or facilities to sell them after that so he came up and talked to Benny and me about handling it for him. Benny didn't want to do it, didn't want to risk getting that involved, so I told the importer that I'd deal it off to the street dealers as a kind of middle man.

He'd front me a hundred keys a week. The car would pull into town with 100 kilos in it and I would unload them all and store them and sell them and meet the cat the next weekend and pay him and he'd drop off another hundred kilos, or 25, or whatever he happened to have. This was 1964. The Haight-Ashbury was mostly still a straight neighborhood. The dealing I did then was before it became a place where people carried guns and ripped each other off and that kind of shit. I was dealing but it was all friendly, people would drop by and rap for a while and get loaded and pick up four or five kilos and be on their way. You could front 10 kilos to somebody and they would actually pay you later.

Anyway, one day this friend of mine calls and says he's got a guy in Mexico who has a way that he can guarantee delivery on the other side of the border and provide some Acapulco Gold, really good weed, top of the line herb at that time. We'd been getting weed from some other people who'd been getting it across the border, but their connection dried up, so this guy turned me on to his connection in Mexico. I went down and talked with him and set up a thing. This other buddy of mine and I each put up half the bread and we got the weed and it went smooth, so we started doing this thing in Tijuana pretty regularly. Then from there we started looking for better weed and eventually were doing business in the Guadalajara area. Then, looking for better weed still, we got in farther south into Acapulco and Guerrero, into the Acapulco Gold area.

And that's where I was the past two years.

Chapter Four
1967-1968: The Big Bust

So I had this guy who was bringing in a hundred, hundred-and-fifty kilos a week, just leaving them. When I had them sold and needed more I'd call and three, four days later he'd bring me more. I'd pay him for the ones I'd sold and we were going great guns. That was like about four years ago and there weren't that many people in the San Francisco Bay Area doing a hundred a week then. We were really running around, we did a hundred in three days once. These days, of course, at the right price you could do a hundred in ten minutes! The market is incredible. They can't grow enough weed in Mexico to keep up with demand. I daresay you could sell six hundred kilos just like that, just in San Francisco.

See there's a network of people who all know each other. Every one of about 200 guys who're dealing knows the other hundred and ninety-nine. I've known them all for five years. I know what's happening with them, with their families, with their friends and they know what's happening with me and my family and friends. That's why we mostly don't get busted.

But I got busted once. We attracted a little too much attention. This friend in L.A. was bringing up weed, fronting it to me, and I was selling to a guy in San Francisco who was selling it to another guy who came up from L.A. to score and then took it back to L.A. again. Right! Full circle! But the guy who came up from L.A. to score got busted, so of course the cops, as they always do, offered him a bullshit deal if he turned them on to the guy he was buying from. And the guy's a big enough sap to go for the deal. It's really no deal at all because they tell you "You turn us on to everyone and tell us everything and we'll do what we can for you." Then they give the you like six months in jail and fourteen years of probation reporting once a week or something. Not exactly beautiful at all.

Of course, the first thing you have to do when you're making a deal with the heat is tell on yourself. Then you tell on everyone else. And the guy goes for it. He brings the Feds up, sets up a deal and introduces this Fed — who looked like a cop, I mean he didn't look like anyone you'd be selling any weed to — but anyway, he introduces this Fed to this guy I was selling to. And they bust him, too. And not only does this jerk bring the Feds into it, but he brings along a chick who doesn't know anything about it and gets her busted, too!

See, I had a guy who was working for me, doing my deliveries, I would set it all up and he would do the deliveries and collect the money. He goes to meet the guy from L.A. and he's got about 40 or 50 keys in his truck. I had warned him repeatedly to only do business with the people I've got the deal set up with. Don't do any business if they bring somebody else along, especially if it's somebody you don't know, someone you've never seen before. But he goes to meet the cat from L.A. and not only has that guy brought another guy with him, but another chick that my delivery guy's never seen before either, and he does the delivery anyway! So they bust him. They get him with those 40 or 50 keys and they say to him, "We know you're working for another guy and we know there's a stash and we're going to find it anyway, but if you take us to it we'll go easy on you and easy on your chick." Fine. They haven't got him with enough shit already, 50 kilos, he's got to take them to the stash. Gives 'em the key, signs an entry permission slip and they go in and find another 150 keys and 4,000 hits of acid. So then they've really got him by the nuts. They start turning the screws. "Look, we've got you with more dope than we've ever busted before, it's about time you started talking. We want a signed statement that you're working for this guy because we're going to bust him." They have one fink already, all

32

they need is this one more, and this guy is him. He signs.

Now I know nothing about all of this. I was in bed asleep at 2 a.m. and the doorbell rings. I thought, "Ohhh, what is this?" I mean, who would be at the door at 2 a.m.? So I go down this long flight of stairs to the front door and turn on the porch light and see this cat's silhouette and I say, "Who is it?" and he says "Me." I say "Who's 'me'?"

CRASH! The door bursts open and these six guys with pistols drawn charge in. "Getcher hands up! You're under arrest!" and I say "What for?" and he says "You know what for!" Well, when I got out of bed I wrapped a towel around me because I don't use pajamas or wear underwear in bed, so when I put my hands up, the towel dropped. They grab my arms and handcuff my hands behind my back, so I'm standing there naked in the middle of the hall, handcuffed, and this guy slams me up against the wall, jams his gun in my back and says "You move and I'll blow your guts out." I looked over my shoulder and said, "Hey, man, you got me in the middle of an empty hall, there's nothing here I could grab even if I wanted to, My hands are behind my back, my face is up against the wall, a .38's in my back … what the fuck d'you think I'm gonna do?"

Then they start searching. There was a box of chocolate-covered cherries in the closet with the unopened cellophane wrapper still on it and this guy opens it up and pokes his finger into each candy. I said, "Right, that's where I hide it. I make chocolate-covered cherries." They were incredible. They never did look in the kitchen, they missed about a pound and a half of weed there. They missed a couple of lids in the living room. While they're searching, this buddy of mine, Tim, who worked late and sometimes would drop by to smoke a joint after work, sees the lights on and figures he'll come in and get loaded. He comes in and he gets to the top of the stairs and these two cops, without saying a word to him, come around the corner and grab him. Well. he's a strong cat, and he doesn't know who the hell they are, so he busts loose and pastes one of 'em, knocks him on his ass, busts his lip wide open. I mean, wouldn't you start busting out if two guys you'd never seen before grabbed you out of nowhere? So then four of 'em jump on him and wrestle him down and they're hitting him and one's got his arm in a hammerlock and another one is yelling "Break it! Break it off!"

I'm standing there watching and telling them "Hey, let him up! You've got him! What're you doing?" So then this Fed says "Just put the cuffs on him," because he could see that there were people gathering outside and these two particular cops, San Francisco narcs, are super-pigs, they enjoy crashing through windows and kicking people's doors down, they dig it. They would never come to the door with a warrant and knock. I mean, they go to bust a hippie, right, and there had never been a case at the time in San Francisco where they'd ever busted a hippie who had ever even thought of shooting it out. I mean, the Man is at the door, there's no place to go, just let him in or tell him to go away and get a warrant and then he'll knock the door down. But I mean these two cops dig doing that. The cop who had my friend down in a hammerlock gets up and reaches down and grabs the back pocket of his pants and rips the ass out of the pants. Tim turns and looks at him and says, "Did you get your rocks off, motherfucker?"

So they take everybody off and these two Feds put me in the back of this station wagon with one driving and the other sort of leaning over the back seat on the way downtown. He's saying "Well, you want to tell us about it now? There's nobody else around. Now's the time to do yourself some good because we know that you're just dealing this stuff, you're not smuggling it in, so all you have to do is set us up for a border shipment and we'll make it real easy on you." I said, "Hey, do I get a chance to make a phone call?"

34

He says, "Oh, you're gonna be a smart guy, huh?" I said, "I'm going to be as smart as I can. All I want to do is make a phone call. I want to call my bail bondsman, that's all I want to do."

He says, "You know, we got you with a bunch."

I said, "What're you talking about? A bunch of what?"

And the guy swings around, swings his arm like he's going to hit me in the face but stops his fist just short of my face. And he says, "Now you want to tell us about it?"

I said, "Hey, man, do whatever you're going to do, I ain't telling you shit. All I want to do is make a phone call."

We pull up in front of the Federal Building and there's a truck unloading all these duffle bags full of weed onto the pavement. I'm sitting there thinking, "All this beautiful stuff and the Man's got it." And the guy pulls up and sits there while they unload and then turns around to me and says "You want to give us a hand upstairs with your stuff?" And I say "I didn't bring anything with me." He says "Your bags are over there." "Bags!" I said. "I've never seen those bags before." And I hadn't, I had never seen that weed. They got it at the stash house and they told me the address and I said "I don't know where that is. I've never been there in my life." I hadn't either. I had someone else rent the place and somebody else was doing the pickups and drop-offs. I didn't even know the address before the Feds told me.

So we go upstairs and they book and fingerprint me and take photos and all that. We get finished with that and I'm washing up and the cat in charge of fingerprinting is their soft-touch man. They've been threatening me, threatening to hit me and saying things like "We got ways of making you talk" and jive shit like that and now this guy is the soft-touch man. He comes on with stuff like "How long you been smoking weed? I'd sort of like to try it sometime." I said "Smoke? I don't smoke. Weed? What do you mean?" He says "You know, marijuana, how long have you been smoking marijuana?" and I said "What're you talking about? I don't smoke marijuana." All kinds of silly games like that.

Then they bring the hard sell on again. They take me into this room and sit me down and they have all these kilos stacked up on a big, long table. They sit me in the corner and all these Feds form a ring around me, put their feet up on chairs, their elbows on their knees, and the head man comes in and sets himself up and puts his face real close to mine and says, "Y'know, you got a real stink on your hands here."

I just went "(Sniff-sniff). Ah, yeah, I think I smell shit all right."

He says "Maybe you'd like to tell us about it now."

I said, "Man, all I want to do is make my phone call."

So finally they decided they weren't going to hold me on Federal charges and shipped me downtown to city jail. We got busted at 2 a.m. and it was 7 or 8 before I got a chance to make my phone call. They questioned me off and on for hours. They'd let me sit for a while, then bring me in and start grilling me, then let me sit some more, then more questioning. But I finally got to call my bail bondsman and a lawyer and get out of jail. Then I went to court for over a year, had three trials. We finally finished. My lawyer separated the big quantity from the small quantity and tried the big quantity first. I got not guilty in a jury trial. Then we tried the small quantity and got a hung jury. Then they offered a deal. If I'd plead guilty to possession of one joint, it'd be 60 days in County Jail and three years' probation, and they'd cut the chicks loose. So I did it. We might have got another hung jury if we'd gone on with it, or we could have gotten convicted or an acquittal. But if they convicted me at trial they would sock it to me because they'd missed on the big quantity and they'd wanted to nail me on that. When they didn't, they went for the small quantity but when they got the hung jury their confidence was shaken. They weren't sure they could get a conviction. And they want to get some kind of conviction to make it look like they have it together. So that's how it all worked out.

But jail was too much. I don't ever want to go to jail again! If it ever comes up again that I have to go to jail, I think I'd split, I wouldn't stay around. Because jail is *foul*, man. That door clangs shut behind you and there's nowhere else to go and nothing to do.

And the quarters! The first thirteen days I was there I slept right on the floor of the fifth floor of the jailhouse. The fifth floor is just like the seventh floor is just like the second floor. On each side of the corridor there's a bank of cells, one bunk to each cell. The cells are about five feet wide, ten feet high and maybe eight feet deep. They all have one window almost the full width of the cell and one door with big steel bars on it. In each cell there are two men, one sleeping on a bunk (he was there first) and one sleeping on the floor on a blanket. That's all he has, one blanket, period, on the floor. The new arrivals sleep out in the corridor between the cells on mattresses on the floor. If you could see the mattresses, you wouldn't want to touch 'em, much less sleep on them. Blood-stained, smelly, dirty, funky motherfuckers. And you never get the same mattress twice because you turn in your mattress at four in the morning. You get to keep your blanket. From then on you have the rest of the day with nothing to do but sit on your blanket. Absolutely nothing to do. If somebody's got a radio you're really lucky. There's no ping-pong, no recreational facilities, no rehab, nothing. You just sit there and that's all there is to do. At nine-thirty at night they bring the mattresses back and everybody scrambles for mattresses. It's a scrum for the mattresses. You line up and whoever's not afraid to bump somebody else might get a clean mattress. Ninety-seven percent of the guys don't get a clean mattress. Guys get in fights over them.

And the food, the food is incredible, and inedible. Potato soup with lots of onions and nothing else. I mean, water, potatoes and onions, period. And the same coffee for dinner you had for breakfast with a little added to it. I saw sides of beef, truckloads, come in but I never saw a string of beef to eat. Oops, excuse me, I did see a string of beef in some soup once, but I also saw guards carrying out a lot of big packages.

And first of all, A-Number 1, the blacks are in charge and there's no question in anybody's mind about that. The guards are afraid of them, not individually but collectively. So all the cats who have all the advantages on a floor are black cats. One-hundred percent. So anybody who can get next to those cats is all right. I get along with people really well, so I'm still sleeping on the floor but I've got money. I can't spend as much money as I have in that jail. Because I can only possibly spend about $5 a day at the most. The real medium of exchange is cigarettes, so I'm stocking up on those. When I go to the commissary I buy cartons of cigarettes. I can trade cigarettes for anything. I can trade cigarettes for grass. In the first 10 days I was there I stayed stoned as a motherfucker. I had four or five joints a day. A pack of cigarettes per joint, sometimes two or three packs. And the black cats were the ones who got the weed into the place. They had a thing going where the people who packaged the denim for making jail clothes would hide the weed in the bolts of denim. They'd shoot it into the jail, it'd go to the tailoring shop where all the workers were spades and they'd get the weed out and sell it. That finally got busted while I was there.

Guards got paid off there, not as much as some other places, from what I heard, but some. I finally ended up in the dormitory — after pulling all kinds of strings and bitching and having my lawyer come out — and I was in the bunk next to the boss spade of the whole jailhouse, a cat named Otis. After I got next to him I had steak sandwiches, eggnog, a drink every once in a while, weed when I wanted it. But the guards would bust you if they could, a pig is a pig is a pig. They'd come around and shine a flashlight in your eyes at night, shit like that, just to harass you.

There were deer on the grounds outside and when I noticed the deer I started thinking a lot about getting out because I could see them just running across the hills and I wanted to follow them. "Let me go run with the deer, please, let me go sleep in the grass, but let me OUT of this fucking jailhouse, man!" I was going crazy! I spent three months there and I should have gotten out sooner but about 10 days before I was supposed to get out a guy threw a softball at me and hit me in the head. So I turned and threw the ball about a hundred yards over the fence. For losing the softball they gave me five days in solitary. They put me in a cell and gave me nothing but bread and water. You are totally isolated. So that extended my stay a bit.

One other thing that happened while I was there, just to show what kind of place it is: a guy accumulated enough material somehow to make a fire to boil some water to throw on a guard. He got the guard, scalded his ass. I'm not normally a malicious guy but I was glad because that guard was just a bastard. I could've strangled him myself. He had been taunting the guy who threw the water. Calling him all kinds of racial slurs. He'd been doing that for a couple of weeks when the guy scalded him.

That spade cat was a really strong guy, he wasn't going to take any shit. Most people in jail realize they're going to have to compromise a little bit and try to slide on through as best they can, but this cat was just "No, man, no, y' can't cut my hair, I'm not going to shave, I'm not going to kiss your ass and I'm not going to say 'yes' when I feel like saying 'no.' And just plain NO, motherfuckers!" They killed him finally. About a week after his sentence was up and he got out they shot him on the street in front of his brother for no real reason. They stopped him on the street to hassle him and he said "No, I'm not doing anything, I'm not going to be hassled." He turned around and was just walking away from them, not even running, mind you, and this pig pulls his gun and shoots him in the head.

And that's just County Jail. It's not even a maximum security state or Federal prison. For contrast, look at the guy we were scoring weed from inside Mexican Federal prison near Guadalajara. Inside the prison he had his own house, his old lady and his kids, a TV set and stereo and telephone. He had cocaine and weed and I'd go there and pay the guard a hundred pesos to let me in to score weed. Mind you, here I am, a gringo walking into a prison in Guadalajara, paying my way in. I'd go in and see this guy, sit down and smoke some weed, sniff some coke, do business, pay him and go back to the gate. The guard would come to the gate and put the kilos in the trunk of the car. Okay, I've heard people say they don't ever want to go to Mexican jail, but an American with the amount of money even the poorest American has can live real well there. If he has enough money, he can even have weekends off. And it doesn't matter who you are, you have the right to have your wife or your girlfriend or whatever come visit because they don't want any raped boys in their prisons and they have good sense about it.

So comparing that with what it was like in good old County Jail, I'd much rather be in jail in Mexico than in County Jail or any other prison up here.

Chapter Five
1968: The Dealing Scene

This is a digression, something that happened as a result of some business I had set up while I was going to court, but it helps show how heavy the dealing scene had become by then. A friend had turned me on to a connection in Tijuana and I'd gone down there with my money and two other guys, it was a three-way partnership at first. We had arranged the whole thing, we went down there, took the chance of going to the connection's house with the money and sat with him while the weed moved across the border. We had arranged a pickup on the other side, for the stuff to be transferred to another car, had arranged all the transportation, all the movement across the border. We delivered it to another guy who sold it and took his own chances on that part. His risk was minimal because he was doing business with people we had all known for a long time, people we trusted. Most of the risk was south of the border. If the cops bust you up north, they might bruise your arm or bloody your nose or something but in Mexico knives and guns happen in a serious way.

So anyway, we'd set it all up and while all this is going on I'm still going to court. I'm jumping on a plane and shooting to San Diego and grabbing a bus and crossing the border and setting it up, getting the weed across and picked up, then flying back up here to go to court. By this time besides me, a friend who was in on this trip to Mexico, Grant, had been busted, other friends of mine had been busted, so they were watching us. We were living over in the country and the cops would sit in front of the house and we'd go someplace and they'd follow us. We'd turn it around and follow them and they'd freak out ... stuff like that. But we never really figured they'd pick us up in Mexico.

We had a bunch of money, eight grand or so, and it

was Tanya and me and Grant and his old lady and we were staying in this hotel with an ounce of hash in the room. We were out cruising around, just killing time and driving from pay phone to pay phone, calling people to line this whole thing up for the border crossing, and we got stopped for a traffic violation, an illegal left turn or something. There's a warrant out for Grant, who's in the back seat, and we know that, so I get out of the car and walk back to the police car so they won't look at Grant or ask for his I.D. I'm standing back there at the front of the patrol car and the cop is questioning me while the other cop is in the patrol car checking my license. I hear the voice on the patrol car radio ask "Can those people hear you?" The cop looks at me to see if I flash on it but I'm just steadily looking the other way (with my ears big and round!) and he says "No, they can't hear me."

Then the cat on the radio says "Just give 'em a ticket for their infraction and let 'em be on their way because customs is following them and doesn't want us to disturb it." I thought to myself "Oh, yeah? Thanks for telling us!" I get back in the car and slowly drive on down the street and turn a couple of corners and sure enough, we have a tail, bigger'n shit! So we go back to the motel and casually go to our room and casually close the door and grab this hash and split it four ways and eat it. It's either that or throw it away. We clean everything up, check out the room to see if there are any seeds or anything and sit down to figure out what's next.

We know they're following us but we don't know if the room is bugged, we figure it probably is since they're following us this far and this close, so from then on the only time we talk about business is in a pay phone booth we know we've never used before and far enough from the car that if there's a bug on the car it won't pick up our conversations. Or we turn on the car radio so loud that it'll drown out the conversation. Because one of the top professional debuggers said that loud rock music will muffle a whispered conversation completely.

So we're on a big trip about it and we decide that this chick in Mexico is going to have to take the weed across the border. We figure they're really watching us, and we have to have it set up so that if she gets popped entering the U.S., someone will be covering her and she'll be taken care of immediately, bailed out and so on as soon as possible. Plus we wanted to be sure she wasn't screwing around. Everybody had to be in the right place at the right time doing the right things.

So we're going from phone to phone, super-paranoid, and I didn't know if it was possible for them to bug phones that quickly, but I wasn't going to risk using the same phone twice. We'd drive to a pay phone and they'd be right behind us. We'd stop at a phone booth and they'd park a block away and wait. They didn't even seem to be trying to be secretive about it, or if they were trying, they were really bad at it. But we started running out of pay phones because we were making quite a few calls. So we were driving way out by the outskirts of this little community on the desert near San Diego where there was always a pay phone and somehow we made a turn that they didn't and we lost them, just accidentally.

Pretty soon here come two helicopters flying low and criss-crossing each other and finally one of 'em spots us and hovers over us. The other one splits and two cars come across the desert zig-zagging along, we see their dust trails coming toward us and as soon as they're in sight of us, the other chopper splits. It was far out! They were *on* us!

So somebody had to take the bread across the border to get this business done. There was no way for either me or Grant to change our appearance enough to make any significant difference in being able to slip these people, but Tanya and Grant's chick both had some straight

43

clothes and wigs and stuff, so we drove up to a restaurant near the border. The ladies went into the restroom, changed clothes and put on wigs, separated and went across the border, met each other on the other side, grabbed a cab and did a number to be sure they weren't being followed. They really knew downtown Tijuana. There are a lot of little places where you can go into a market building or something and come out of any of 20 doors on two or three levels. That makes an ideal place to ditch somebody because you can slip into the crowd, walk around multiple areas and then go out another door and just disappear.

So they slipped across, did that number, got the money to the man on the other side and while we were waiting for them we went to car washes because I knew the cops were going to follow us to see if they could figure out the connection. And if they couldn't figure anything out, they were going to stop us and really go through us. Because they knew why we were there and I knew there could be flecks of weed on the carpet or a seed in a heater vent or something that they could use to bust us. So we went to four car washes: vacuum it, wash it, vacuum it, wash it, vacuum it, wash it till it was spotless. We had a roach clip that had some weed tar on it and I got a piece of steel wool and polished it till there wasn't one speck. I got all of Grant's I.D. papers and took a couple of camera lenses apart and put his papers in there and put the cameras back together. He could say he'd lost his papers in Mexico if it came to that.

Then we picked up the chicks at the border. They'd gotten the money to the connection down there and it was all set. What happened was, they took the bread to a guy who had a woman drive a car across with all the weed, park it in downtown San Diego, then call the connection to let him know she'd dropped it off. Then he called our chick and told her where the car was and that she could go pick it up. We'd done this dozens of times and it had always

44

worked.

So we headed north for San Francisco but it was getting to feel cramped with four of us in this sports car that I had so when we got to L.A., we decided to go to the airport and ship the baggage. We knew they were following us and would follow us to the airport and think the weed was in the luggage. So we sent the luggage off and started back up the freeway toward San Francisco. We get about five miles out of L.A. and all of a sudden I realize there's a car right behind us who at this point is making no pretensions of not following us. He's there, staring at us real hard. Then another car passes him and comes up beside us and pulls in front of us and begins to slow down. I think to myself "Okay, one more!" and sure enough, another car pulls alongside us and they just force us to slow down and stop off the road. This guy walks up and I roll down the window and he says "Where ya going?"

I say San Francisco and he says "Where ya been?"

I said "Why play games? You were following us, right? You're not stopping us for a traffic violation, what do you want?"

"Well," he says, "we'd like to go through your car if you don't mind."

I say I don't and he says they want to do it at a service station just up the road, so we go there and they go through the car. Seven of them were over and under and into that car in every possible way. They took me and Grant to the restroom and thoroughly searched us. They searched the ladies' purses and found the freight bill from the airport. The guy who found it just went "FLASH!" When I saw him copying the freight bill numbers I said "You mean you guys lost us over by the airport and let us get that luggage out of town?" He just looked at me like if looks could kill. It was a mind-blower because this was Feds and they had a bunch of guys on us and lost us by accident at a critical point when we weren't even trying to lose 'em! I thought it was really funny. Plus it shows how hard it is to get around LAX.

Oh, and Tanya started getting salty, asking them what they were doing and what did they want with us and what do you think we're doing and one guy says "Your husband's not exactly an angel, you know." She says "What do you mean?" and I said "Baby, they know who we are."

But they didn't know who Grant was. They looked in the camera cases, but never thought of opening the lenses so they didn't find his papers and couldn't verify who he was. And there was that warrant out for him. It's not like they're jerks, they're college-educated dudes, not average pigs. But they didn't think of taking off the lenses. So there's a lot of stuff that gets by them just because they don't think of everything. And they didn't have a matron so they couldn't really search the chicks.

But I don't know. They must have thought we were into something else because the places they were looking weren't places where you'd look for weed. They must have thought we were into something with coke or smack or something like that. While they were searching us the stuff was coming across the border. It was pretty easy then, but not anymore, not the way they go through cars now. We always drove it across before but we finally had to change because they were getting too hip to that, they were really starting to nail people.

So anyway, I was going to court and getting this partnership set up and then I went to jail. But I had everything set up before I went in. I took Tanya and another guy, Barry, down there and introduced them to the connection and educated them about how to handle a movement across the border. And Grant would handle things up here. So I go to jail thinking everything's going well because the reports I am getting during visiting hours and in code in letters say it's all getting done. But I come

46

out of jail and find out that Grant is holding all the cash. He's telling me I don't need to worry, he's going to take care of me. As soon as he says that, I think "Oooo-kay, what the fuck is going on? He's going to take care of me, I don't have to worry about the bread, I'm just supposed to relax and ..." I think, well, maybe its possible. I'd been in jail for a while and went through a lot of changes behind that and I think well, he's my friend, so maybe ... and at first I don't say anything. I ask him for a couple of hundred dollars and he gives me five hundred.

During three months before I went to jail, the operation brought in fifteen or twenty thousand dollars profit plus all costs and incidentals. We lived damned good. We did a lot of jetting around and always had a lot of dope to smoke, the refrigerator was always full, we had plenty of everything. We had cars, Porsches and Jaguars all over the place. Then I was in jail for two months, and when I got out I had to assume it had made more money on the trips across the border while I was in jail. But the first time I talk to him about it he tells me he owes me six or seven grand, which is about half of what I figure it should be. And when I start asking him about it he doesn't want to pay me, he starts giving me a stall: he left the bread with some chick because it was safer with her but she was out of town and wasn't going to be back for a while. It started sounding real suspicious to me.

But I was just out of jail, I didn't really want to worry about it too much. We drove up to visit my folks. Tanya had had the car all cherried out while I was in jail, had an FM radio installed, so we were just cruising around having a good time. We rented a place up the coast so we could just lay back, I could fool around with the camera, take pictures and enjoy my freedom. So I didn't really stress over the bread, I had my lady, my wheels, some weed to smoke and a place to groove around in and enjoy my dog and we could walk on the beach and just normal stuff like that, so I was happy for a while.

But then I started thinking about the bread and started getting hot on the issue. So then it comes down to a story that Grant got burned for the bread by fronting some stuff to someone who didn't pay up and so on. So I think, "Well, okay, now it's out, he's admitted that he fucked up, that he fronted the weed out and got burned and he says he's going to make it up." And I can see he seems to be working on it so I think he probably will take care of it. But then I run into this woman who's a friend of a friend of his and she's worked for us in the business, ran errands and made phone calls and stuff like that, and I see her carrying a bag with lots of cash in it. This chick is a chick who cannot lie. She's a really beautiful chick, a simple chick, I mean she's competent, she can lie to the heat or something like that, but if it's a friend, somebody close to her like we were, and you questioned her, she'd just have to tell the truth. Or at the very least she'd say "I can't really talk to you about it, you'll have to talk to him," or something like that. So when I saw the bread, I said, "Betty, how much cash you carrying there?" She said about seven thousand dollars. I asked her where she was going with it and she said "I'm taking it to Grant."

I was pissed! Because he's been steadily telling me he's broke and here she is with his seven grand. I'm thinking that even if it's money he's paying to somebody for something they fronted to someone for something they fronted him to sell in order to pay me, still, if he's doing business in seven-grand chunks you know he's making some thousands in there somewhere. And he's been giving me fifty bucks here, a hundred bucks there, kind of stringing me along. I'm salt pissed.

So I jump in the car. He's been hanging out at the Straight Theatre, which I later found out a whole bunch of bread went into that fucking rathole, and I never even got the consideration of a free door pass for my five-thousand investment or whatever it was. Anyway, he's down there and she's taking the bread to him there so I said, "I'll follow you and talk to him about it."

And I'm ready for the cat, man, really ready, because when I was in jail and had nothing to do I got all tensed up because, for one thing, it was the first time in a long, long time, many, many years that I was deprived of my woman. So I concentrated on other things. I quit smoking, started doing pushups and pull-ups and that kind of stuff and when I came out of that place, I was solid, like a fucking rock. It was also partly because when I went in I was a pretty boy and there are lots of pretty boys that get raped in jail,, and that wasn't going to happen to me. Anybody wants to try that with me, I'm going to make it very difficult for them. So when I got out I was really strong. Then we spent time in the country where I'd get up in the morning and chop wood for a couple of hours and walk five miles to the beach to throw chunks of lumber for the dogs, then come back and chop more wood, dig in the garden, that kind of stuff. Grant's been running around in the city taking heavy psychedelics, shooting methedrine, dissipating and probably worrying a lot, so if I wanted to grab him and bend him around a lamp post it would have been pretty easy.

But he gives me five hundred and another stall and then keeps on stalling and stalling and I hear more and more about how well he's doing but I'm not getting any of the bread I'm supposed to be getting. So I'm in the city and I find out that he's running around with like grams of acid that he owns, worth at that time something like four to five grand a gram. That was it. When I heard that, I was sitting in some people's living room, barefooted, a T-shirt on or something and it was cold and rainy outside but when I heard that I got up, walked over to my coat, took my hunting knife out of the pocket and stuck it in my back pocket and walked out the door and through the driving rain about 10 blocks over to his house. I was ready to bust the door down if he was home. I'd had it, I had my knife and I was going to use it, I was going to kick down the door and beat the shit out of him and slit his throat. But luckily for both of us he wasn't home.

It just shows the direction the business had gone since the simple early days. It was one more thing that finally made me want out of the business, that stress of getting to that point with people, especially a guy who was supposed to be my friend and who I'd trusted. It was a bummer.

Chapter Six
1968: A Brush With Danger

Year before last was the first time I went to Zihuatanejo. That was when I met Domingo — that motherfucker! But at the time he seemed cool and like he knew what he was doing, how to set up a trip and score some righteous weed. I met him through a buddy of mine who was just traveling around Mexico. He'd met someone who told him to go to Zihuatanejo, that it was groovy, and he went there and got a taste of the weed and wrote me that I ought to check it out, said it was really far out dope. So I went down there and he knew a cat who was dealing weed from Domingo. We were living in a little rented palapa out by the point where the point of the bay comes out at the ocean. We were on the ocean side.

This guy brought Domingo out so we could talk about setting something up and that's how I met Domingo. The far out thing was that while I was negotiating through this other guy with Domingo, Domingo was working for us at the palapa, cutting trails and digging latrines, going through the palapa to kill scorpions and tarantulas, things like that. And he was dealing joints on the beach, which is just something that goes on down there. It's a hell of a lot easier to earn money that way than to grow corn or pick coconuts or any of that.

So I see that there's really good weed there, I mean really outasight, and it looks like I can get it without too much hassle. I start setting up transportation and it looks like everything is cool but I end up trying to work with this guy who's one of the biggest bummers I've ever run across in the dope business, a jerk beyond belief! It's like somewhere around the middle of July, still the rainy season down there, and I planned to go to this cat Frank who had done the thing before, he had a camper unit of some kind with some real straight-looking people driving it and good

51

stash space built in, hard to find and all that, and he'd gotten a couple of loads across the border before. But he was a weird cat, I really didn't dig him because he seemed like a cop. He was a big, heavy, pot-bellied guy, real straight looking, and on a super ego trip about "Oh, yeah, we'll get it across, I'll take care of that," and all this line about "no problem with money, we got everything covered," and so on. So I didn't like him, but talking to people who had done business with him, it seemed like he could do it.

He was already involved with some other people in Mazatlan, he was supposed to do some trip there. But when he got a taste of the weed that I brought back from going down to check things out, he decided he would do our trip, too. So he was supposed to go to Mazatlan and stay with the people there with his camper. My brother Samuel would go there with him and as soon as he got there and everything was ready Samuel would shoot down to where I was in Guerrero. As soon as we were ready for everything to be picked up, Samuel would fly back up to Mazatlan and tell Frank everything was ready and Frank would come down to pick up the weed and we'd be done.

Okay, so I fly to Acapulco and they're supposed to be on their way driving to Mazatlan. I rent a Jeep and drive to Zihuatanejo, back to the palapa, which is just rock walls three and a half feet high with openings for doors and a thatched roof. There's a hammock and a hot plate with electricity from a wire run across the floor of the jungle. It works as long as the wild pigs don't trip over the wire and bust it. Or if there's too much power being used downtown and there's not enough juice to make it over the hill. Or unless someone pulls the plug at the other end, that kind of scene. Same thing with water. I have "city water," which is a joke, it's just a plain old garden hose run across the jungle. Deer would come through in the middle of the night and step on the hose and break it and I'd have to track down the leaks and tape them up. But I have "city water," which doesn't mean anything except that there's no other water on this hill and the only other way to get water is to haul it from a well out in the swamp. I mean you would never want to drink that, you would just take one look at it and know it was poison. You pour it in a cup and it could be a black cup but that water would be blacker than the black cup, blacker by far. And besides that, it's technicolor water, little red things floating in it. You just would not want to drink it.

So those are the living conditions. And I've got maybe 10 or 12 grand, in cash because everything's cash in the business. We're working on a couple of deals, one of them with Grant who's setting up something with a Mexico City college student who's down for the summer and one through this guy who turns out to be Domingo. I met Grant quite a few years back when he was one of the first cats around the Haight-Ashbury, when we were all living there before it became a big scene. He was just a cat who hung around, he lived in one of the famous early Haight-Ashbury psychedelic pads with this lady who had a little daughter. A couple of the early articles on the hippie trip in San Francisco in the newspaper originated from her place. Cats like Paul Butterfield used to stay there when they were in town, that kind of scene.

So when I went to jail Grant worked with Tanya to keep the trip together that we had at the border. Then he got bummed out by it and split. He hitch-hiked across the country and worked his way to the Bahamas for a while, then the next thing I hear from him is the letter telling me to check out the weed in Zihuatanejo. Grant's just a very far-out guy. For example, he decided he would learn to play the organ, but instead of starting to practice that, he set about figuring out the mathematics of music. When he had that figured out, he decided he had music down and it would be nothing more than exercising manual dexterity to actually play music, so he went off on some other mind trip. He's very far out, super-intelligent. So he was working with me down there, but he's so abstract that it just blows your mind to be around him, a really abstract kind of cat.

At one point we had a house in Zihuatanejo and a house in Acapulco. We were scoring in Zihuatanejo and bringing it down to Acapulco to brick up and ship out. He was staying at the house in Acapulco and he would do things like burning all his clothes. Then he started bitching because he didn't have any clothes, so I took him downtown and bought him a bunch of clothes. The very next afternoon he ripped the sleeves out of the shirts and cut the legs off the pants, then started bitching again about not having any clothes!

He built this *thing*. The original purpose was supposed to be to magnetize steel balls along an axis around a box and push them toward the center of the box, then all those magnets would come together and line themselves up to make random kinds of patterns, like strings of molecules. It was going to be a children's game. So he set out to build an electromagnet for this thing. It covered an the entire floor of the maid's quarters. We didn't have a maid because we didn't want the maid living there and seeing what we were doing, so she came a couple of times a week and it was still a big hassle to keep her away from the grass. But Grant had this thing laid out, it must have been six or seven feet square, with all these wires and lights to test the circuits and brackets to hold the pieces of metal to see what kind of magnetic force he was getting, and this circuit that when he turned a switch on over here a blue light would go on over there and a red light over here and there'd be clicking sounds and ... I mean, it was just ... weird.

So one day this maid, who's really a simple chick — a 15-year-old Indian from the jungle who's in the city working, trying to figure out what's happening with all this

54

civilization business — one day she walks into what used to be her quarters and here's this cat with all his clothes half ripped off, laying this stuff out with all this stuff happening, the room practically humming, and it's a hundred degrees and he's sweating over this incredible thing ... I can't even imagine what she thought. He just blew people's minds on a regular basis.

And Grant had a thing about breaking glass. He'd get so wrapped up in trying to figure out the universe ... he had a theory of an expanding and contracting spiral universe that about six months later was published in Scientific American by some other cat. I mean he had all the equations and everything, exactly the same. So Grant's not just jiving, he's really *there*! But sometimes he gets to a point where he's right on the verge of figuring out something complex but can't quite get on it, can't quite grasp it, and he gets *frantic*! He would smoke opium and weed all day long and just be going "Buzz-buzz! Zing-zing!" and walking all over the house, pacing, couldn't sit still. So one morning I wake up to the sound of glass breaking in the patio. I think "What in hell's going on?" and I look out the window and there's Grant in his shorts and he's got every piece of glass in that house stacked up: half a dozen five-gallon water bottles, ashtrays, cups, saucers, plates, every glass in the house, pieces of pottery, everything! He has 'em all lined up across the courtyard and is methodically picking up one piece at a time and SMASHING it against the wall! I mean all the light bulbs in the house, anything that was glass, he broke to bits. Every last motherfucking piece. And then swept it all up and put it in the garbage can and came in the house and smoked a joint. And he did that two or three times while we were there. I'd go out and buy a whole new set of glass for the house and three weeks later I'd come back and there'd be just a pile of rubble. He finally totally freaked out and had to come back.

vay, we were setting these deals up and we did
, really stupid., something that I never should
. happen. We decided to score this whole large
.nt at one time, five-hundred kilos all at once instead
splitting the transaction into two separate deals so that
we wouldn't get ripped off. I mean it was a lot of money to
carry out into the sticks for the first time ever doing
business with these people. But anyway, Grant's got this
thing set up where we're supposed to go to Petetlan, about
35 miles south of Zihuatanejo, and take a cab five miles
back up toward Zihuatanejo and then a couple of miles off
the highway, then walk about eight miles inland from there.
And we're carrying all this packaging material, boxes of
masking tape, wrapping paper, plastic overwrap, all the
parts to construct a press to make bricks. We're supposed
to hike to a house there and they'll bring the weed down,
and we'll pay them for half of it, then brick it all up and
take it on burros out to where the truck can get to us to pick
it up, and as soon as the truck comes, we'll pay them the
other half. The idea being to make them think that the other
half of the bread is with the people in the truck, so we
weren't carrying the whole amount with us. But it turned
out not to be enough precaution.

So we're leaving Petetlan, which I'd never heard of,
turns out it's a little town 12 miles from the coast and really
hot and primitive, about 5,000 people live there, but it's a
5,000-person village, not a town. There's no tourist traffic
there, they make gold jewelry there, really beautiful and
incredibly cheap. Filigree gold earrings this long and this
wide, beautifully worked, peacocks and doves worked into
them in patterns, for like 75 or 100 pesos, which is like six
and a half U.S. dollars, something like that. And it's solid
gold, not jive gold. They sell these same earrings in the
marketplace in Guadalajara for 20, 25 bucks a pair and
that's considered cheap. In Mexico City they're like double
that and in the U.S. I don't know what you'd have to pay

for them, probably $79 or $80, something like that. So it's an industrial village, not a tourist town. There are *no* gringos in this town, zero. The only gringos that come here are here to score weed, everybody knows that, everybody but me — until I get there and take a look around.

Grant and I meet Domingo there and go check into our hotel because we're supposed to spend the night so we can go out early in the morning with plenty of time to travel in daylight to get our business done. When we check into the hotel I get some really weird vibrations off this lady who's running the place, like she's wondering what's happening with this gringo in Levis and a denim jacket and a cowboy hat and a Zapata mustache, pulling out a bundle of thousand-peso notes in order to get the hundred-peso notes to pay for the room, and, ah, just being totally uncool. But we stay there for the night and get up early in the morning and go outside and man, I can feel it already: everybody in town when we walk by has us pinned! They know what's happening. I'm thinking, "Oh, man, I don't like this." I'm looking around, digging the church, trying to look like somebody who's wandering through while traveling or something.

Plus I'm thinking it would be a really bad idea to take a cab out to the drop-off spot because cab drivers are the universal snitches, anywhere in the world. If you want to do something private, you don't want to let any cab driver know what you're doing. And you can't pay 'em off because if you lay some bread on 'em they'll know there's more. So I ask Domingo "You sure you know what you're doing?" He tells me everything's cool, he knows these people really well and so on — all this being a fairly difficult conversation because like two weeks before that I didn't know but two words of Spanish, "si" and "adios." and here I am trying to communicate some fairly complex things ... HA! you had to be there!

But I think I've got it straight, though I really don't

like it. But I'm also thinking maybe I'm just being paranoid and chickenshit, you know, like: "Come on, where are your guts? You're probably getting cold feet just when it's starting to happen." Because that happens in the business all the time. You're about to do one of these things and just when it's about to come down there's this moment of "Wow, man! I sure hope I got it covered because what we're doing is really dangerous." I go over everything in my mind and it seems all right. I'm carrying half the bread and we're not carrying any weapons yet at this time, we're not thinking that way at all, because at that time we'd been doing business before, we did kilos out of Tijuana, kilos out of Guadalajara, out of San Blas, and it was all fairly civilized. I'd seen a couple of guns before but not on anyone who looked like they were thinking about using them.

Okay, we get in this red taxicab and ride out of town and he drops us and we start walking, and I mean we walk a *bunch*. We walk across streams, we walk up hills and climb over barbed-wire fences and walk through cornfields ... to the point where I'm totally lost! The only way I have of having any idea which direction is which is by where the sun is. Other than that I have no fucking idea how to get back through this route, none, zilch.

We finally get to this place where we're supposed to meet this other Indian. There's a little stream running by and dense jungle all around and a little clearing with a tree in it, so we sit down and throw down all this stuff we're lugging on our backs and Domingo goes off to look for this cat we're supposed to meet. He's gone for maybe 15, 20 minutes and he comes back with this guy and they're maybe 20 or 30 yards from us when all of a sudden they both break into a dead fucking run. I think "Shit! What's going on?" I jump up and as Domingo runs past he yells "Federales! Come on!" And this other Indian cat is running too, so Grant and I get up and take off. Stupidly, for some reason, trying to carry all our stuff. But we're losing ground so finally we throw it all down and just run.

I'm running and Domingo's right in front of me and Grant's a little behind me and for some reason the other Indian cat is *behind* Grant. I think "That's really weird," because Grant's not really an athlete and this other cat is a hills cat, he's used to hard work and traveling through hard country, I can tell by just looking at him. But he's behind Grant and I'm thinking "Oh, man, this is really starting to stink!" Then at one point Domingo stops and holds down a barbed-wire fence for me and I dive over the fence and him and me shoot on through this cornfield and I lose track of Grant but I'm thinking "Baby, if you can't keep up, ain't no use in both of us getting killed!"

Until I hear Grant *scream*! I stopped. Domingo realized I'd stopped and said *"Venga! Venga! Venga!"* — come on, come on, come on! — he's like we'll worry about whoever they got in a minute, but let's get out of danger first, that's the vibe I'm getting from Domingo. But I couldn't do it, man. I turned around and started back into this cornfield and I just barely reach the edge of this field we just ran through when a fucking rifle butt hits me square in the mouth, POOOWWW! And I just … just blackness, down I go. Then the guy jabs the rifle butt in my stomach a couple of times and stands back and holds the gun on me and says something in Spanish like "Get up!" and I think "Aw, shit!"

They take me back to the little clearing and they've got Grant there, down on the ground with about five Federales standing around pointing guns at him. This guy marches me into the clearing. There must have been eight or nine Federales and they start asking us "Where's the dope? Where's the marijuana?" We pretend we don't understand any Spanish figuring the less we say right now, the better off we are. As I think back on it now, that was probably a mistake, but we pretend not to understand and this guy's making gestures like smoking a joint and spreading his arms out and saying *"Donde? Donde esta?"* Where is it? And they've got the other Indian, too.

They start frisking us and they take everything out of our pockets. In my pocket I'm carrying 2,500 dollars in peso notes, so they take that and they're *very* happy about that, but then they start looking for more. After they've searched Grant and me they start looking for more and they're very insistent, so I know that they know there's supposed to be some more bread, the other 2,500 we're supposed to pay for the second half of the weed we're supposed to get, I know they somehow know that. So they beat the shit out of us for a while but we don't tell them anything. Then they beat the shit out of this other Indian we were meeting but it seems like they're pulling it, like they hit him in the stomach with a rifle butt but he sort of sucks in his gut and goes "UNH!" and falls down before the butt actually hits him, and slaps the rifle butt at the same time, stuff like that. It doesn't look to me like they're really hitting him.

I mean they beat the shit out of us, man! Eight cats just wailing on us with rifle butts in the stomach and head and in the groin, too, if you didn't protect yourself. I missed that one, fortunately. So they search us a little more and then notice that I have a ring on, and they searched the Indian and found a little bit of opium on him, and then they get us up and march us a little way and then sit us down again and crack us again with their rifle butts. But they didn't speak any English whatsoever so Grant and I were able to get a few words to each other in English about what we were going to talk about and what we weren't, and so forth. So when they pointed us to the cornfield we looked at each other and flashed on what was probably going to happen: "Look, if they're going to do it, we're going to take it standing up, not freaking out, because that's our best shot." So we started walking toward the cornfield and I whispered "Baby, when we hit that cornfield we got some cover, so get it on, man, straight-ahead get it on!" And as soon as we hit the edge of the field, we started running, just running as fast as we could.

But I couldn't resist taking a look back, y' know, sort of like if it's going to happen maybe I better see it happen. So I shot a glance back and saw them shoot the other Indian. Then I just turned my eyes straight ahead and ran blindly. I heard three or four more shots and I don't know if they were meant for us. I didn't hear any bullets coming through the cornstalks like I figured I would if they were trying to shoot us and missed, so I don't know if they were just having fun celebrating or actually trying to kill us. Because obviously they'd been informed on the basis of they were going to split the take with this Indian cat, then killed him. Whatever it was, we weren't stopping to find out.

And the other 2,500 dollars that Grant had glued inside the lining of his shoes, they never found because they never took his shoes off. I don't know why, because people carry weapons in their shoes, but they never looked there. They probably wouldn't have found it anyway because he'd taken the linings of the shoes out and put the money in and glued the linings back down. So he dug that out of his shoes later, but we weren't even thinking about that right at that point, we were just blindly running for our lives.

Chapter Seven
Just A Tough Gig

We didn't stop running for a long time and we had no idea where we were going. We knew we were basically heading west and that's all we knew. Finally we came out onto this road and there's a man and his wife and their kids coming along this small, dusty dirt road in an oxcart. And I mean we suddenly ran out onto this road, having no business there. We were tore up, bleeding, we were a couple of beat-up cats. We were starting to heave blood and we'd been running through the jungle and tearing over barbed-wire fences, so our hands and faces were all torn up, we were bleeding and black-eyed from the beatings we took, but as soon as we hit this road, we just PSSSSH! ... calm.

We must've looked like I don't know what to this couple. Two gringos, all torn up out in the middle of nowhere and we walk up to this oxcart and ask them the way to Petetlan and the farmer doesn't bat an eye, he's just blank, like this happens every day, he's going to do what has to be done and no more, just don't involve him and his family too deeply. He just points down the road, and we head off that way until finally we got to the main highway and flagged down a pickup with a whole family in it. We told 'em we needed a ride to Petetlan and they just said "Okay, jump in the back," nothing more, nothing less.

We got into Petetlan and people flashed on us. They'd seen us leave and now here we were again, and they knew what had happened: we went out there and got our little gringo butts whipped. They thought it was funny! They'd be smiling as we walked past. So we had to go to the telephone office because Tanya was waiting for us in a hotel in Acapulco that was sort of command central. We called her and said we were catching a bus to Acapulco and would be there at a certain time and to meet us. She said

"What's going on?" I just said I didn't want to go into it right then.

We caught an earlier bus than we thought we could get so we know we're going to miss her when we get there, but we don't care, we just want to get out of Petetlan because we have no idea what may happen now, we just know that we got away and we're going to keep going. So we get back to Acapulco and get off the bus and we're a couple of torn-up motherfuckers. We don't want to go back to the hotel where Tanya is because we don't know if the heat is following us, so we figure we'll check into another hotel. But what are our chances of checking into a decent hotel looking like we looked? We tried a half a dozen places and they just said "no way." So finally I left Grant sitting at the curb holding his head in his hands. I went into a market and bought some clothes and changed and went into a barber shop and washed and got myself cleaned up and shaved (and oh, man! Was *that* a painful process!).

So then I was just all bruised looking but neat and clean and we finally got into a hotel on the strip. A guy got us some pain pills and we had a few drinks and started pulling ourselves together and decided we better go to the hospital. We got x-rayed and got our ribs taped up, which didn't cost much because medical care there doesn't cost that much. We were in the hospital for a while, we had internal bleeding and when that leveled off, it started to piss me off. I'd just lost $2,500 plus maybe another thousand already spent in expenses, and a lot of people were counting on me to come home and show them a profit. We decided to rent a place in Acapulco and get it back together, but be more cautious this time, real slow and careful. So we did that and started putting together another try.

At one point we got a thing set up with this old cat in Acapulco, Pablo, a musician that I'd scored from on other trips, and about a quarter of what we scored from then on came through him. I met him at a place called La

Huerta, the biggest whorehouse in Acapulco. It's a circular, thatched-roofed, open-sided palapa maybe 200 feet in diameter with a bar and a dance floor with tables and beautiful, lush tropical plants and hundreds of chicks running around, everything from short and fat to tall and thin and anything in between, any kind of trip you want — "You like leather and whips? We got it!" By now I had a go-between to get in touch with Pablo because he was a known dealer and I didn't want anyone to start to tie things together. So another old cat, Luis, who played Mexican folk songs in the red light district, was my go-between.

Luis was a really drifty kind of cat, nobody ever knew where he was going to be at any given time. He might get into a trip playing music with people and if they were buying drinks and tipping and he liked being with them, he might not be around for hours. So I'd go late to La Huerta and sit and wait for him. I'm not a customer of the house, I'm just buying a drink or two and waiting for Luis. Then I'd do my business with him and split. When I first went there chicks started hitting on me like they do all the customers and every once in a while I'd buy one of 'em a drink to kill time but I had to tell them "That's not the reason I'm here." All these women were running around in bikinis and I'd watch the trips they went on, watch all the American tourists coming in. There were lots of Texans who were always hated because they are such slobs, loud and boisterous and gross and so on. So for all the same reasons the Texans say they hate Mexican chicks, the chicks feel the same way about them. But the hippies, man, the girls loved the hippies because half the time the hippies didn't even want to ball 'em, they'd just lay money on 'em and dance and drink and talk, have a good time.

There were also couples that came in, some husband would say to his wife, "Let's go see the whorehouse," and they'd come in and dance and men would start hitting on their wives, then they'd get uptight

64

but try to be broadminded, act like they're really sexually liberated but it's really bothering them. Pretty soon the husbands would make some phony excuse and take their wives and split. I took this Mexican businessman I met and his son to La Huerta and some other places, too, because the cathouses in Acapulco are really something. La Huerta is really kind of like a great open house but there are a couple of other semi-private houses up on the hill that are WHEW! really mind-blowers. They're plush: goldfish ponds and fountains and the chicks aren't in bikinis, they're dressed up in sexy tight stuff and sexy flowing stuff and none of that transparent stuff.

Different people would come down as part of my business trip and they'd want to see the whorehouses. I knew where everything was, so we'd go to the Hilton, then the Dome and Tiberius, and then we'd do the whorehouse scene. We'd go check them all out and they'd decide which houses they liked and which chicks they wanted. Of course, usually by the time we got back to whichever one they decided on, the ladies they'd picked out were already occupied, but second choice in any of those places is better than first choice in almost any whorehouse I've ever seen. I could've fallen in love there, really. I met one gorgeous girl from Guadalajara at a house in Acapulco where they were charging 50 bucks, which is a high, high price. All night was a couple of hundred bucks. This one lady would see me and I'd bring in friends and we'd sit there and drink and she wondered what I was doing, thought maybe I was working for the house bringing customers in. I said no, they were just close friends and I was showing them around. We got to be pretty good friends and she was one beautiful-looking lady. She spoke German, French, English and Spanish really well, just a really groovy chick. I got interested enough in her at one point when I was in Acapulco for a few days shooting back and forth between there and Zihuatanejo setting things up that I invited her up to my hotel after work. She called me at 4 in the morning to come by, but I was really beat because I'd been running around doing business and I had to get up early the next day to go back to Zihuatanejo or something, so I told her we'd get together later. But I never got around to it, just never had the time or something, I don't know. It was too bad because she was beautiful.

But I was going to tell you about this businessman and his son that I met. The dad was about six-feet-five, slender, gray hair, silver-mustached, a well-dressed guy and his son was a young, Jewish, New York sort of junior executive cat staying at a fishing club. They'd left their wives in New York and were hanging out at this one whorehouse a lot, they had the run of the place. They'd get up in the morning and take one of the girls from the whorehouse for the day and maybe drive to the beach, get some sun, go swimming, come back, lay around, ball, go dancing. Their wives think they're down in Mexico catching marlin but all they're catching is a bunch of sweet ass.

I was in a cab with them one day riding to the airport. They were going back to the U.S., I was going down to Mexico City. I'd run around with them for a couple of days, they were groovy, but they didn't know what I did. I'd gotten stoned with them a couple of times, so we all knew we all got high. And I had given them a phony name that I was using down there, so they didn't really know who I was. We're at the airport and one of them says, "You never did tell us, what do you do?" I just laid it on 'em, I said, "I'm a smuggler, that's what I do." The young guy reacted with surprise — and he'd always been after his father to dress a little hipper and not use old slang terms, like he was hip and was going to turn his old man on — but when I said that, his eyes got wider and his mouth dropped open. And the old cat, who was supposed to be so uncool, just looked at me steadily and easy and said

"I thought so." It cracked me up!

But back to the subject: we get this trip set up through Luis and it's cool except he doesn't have a scale. The Indian at the house where we go to pick up the weed, the guy who goes up into the Sierra to connect, doesn't have one either. Now whether he actually didn't have one or they're figuring that if they say they don't maybe they can lighten the load a little bit, is open to question, but anyway this cat tells me before we go over, "Bring your scale." So we've already done that a couple of times and Grant's supposedly going to be there helping me, but I had to be in Zihuatanejo for something else, a deal I had going with Domingo — which is another story, how I got back together with him, which I'll explain in a minute — but I had both deals going at the same time in order to accumulate a big load fast and get out. I'd already been down there too long because of the Petetlan rip-off.

So Grant was in Acapulco and I was heading back to Zihuatanejo to do this other thing, so I said to Grant, "Look: Wednesday you're going to pick up this load, it's supposed to be 100 kilos. Here's the bread for it and here're the two scales. Take 'em both and weigh the load with each of them and split the difference with them if the scales don't agree." I had checked out the scales at a couple of different weights but these were those hang-on, spring scales and sometimes they'd match up at one weight and at another weight they'd be different by two or three or four pounds, which when you're talking about a hundred kilos isn't that much difference.

So I gave Grant the instructions and rented a car for him to make the pickup in, he had the scales, the bread, everything was set up. Then when he went out to do it he got nervous and forgot the scales and freaked out when he got there and wouldn't go back out to the car and get the scales, just threw the cash down and grabbed the weed and split. And shit! For what? It turned out to be only 19 kilos!

Now you tell me that a grown man, 26 or 27 years old who's been dealing weed for a long time and is expounding theories on a spiral, expanding and contracting universe that later appear in Scientific American can't tell the difference just by *feel* between 38 pounds and 200 pounds! Come on, man, it's not possible! So he just really blew it.

We had to go back to them and they said, "Well, we really don't know how much it was, we assume it was correct. You didn't bring a scale, and we told you to bring one, but we'll make up half of it." So we have 20 kilos, I was supposed to get a hundred, so I'm 80 short and I get 40 more. So because of Grant's paranoia and gutlessness, because he panicked, it cost me 40 kilos! And he did that a couple more times, too. So he finally had to go home, he was so freaked out. When he left Zihuatanejo he had gone up there with a rented car to pick up my brother and 18 kilos and he came back with my brother but had refused to let him put the kilos in the car! Which if you knew my brother, man, you'd know it would take somebody really freaked out to try and pull something like that on him, let alone get away with it. So the pieces stayed up there in a *bodega* that we had and it rained on them and they finally just rotted. By the time we could get back with transportation, there was nothing but a little pile of mold and some seeds because that's what happens to weed if it gets wet and just sits.

Plus while all this is happening, this cat Frank, who's supposed to be there with his RV, I get a message from my brother by telegram that I should call Frank. He said Frank was hung up by a storm in Mazatlan. Which turned out to be true, there was a tornado and all the roads were flooded and my brother had tried to make it down to Guerrero and had ended up going through rivers with water practically up over the windowsills, so that hung the cat up.

So then I started talking to Frank on the phone about once every 10 days. Every time we talked, he promised to come down. Finally I decided nothing could happen until he got there. And then *he* could wait while I finalized things. Because I had a couple of things set up that I wasn't sure would work, but I knew they definitely wouldn't work without him and his camper there. But he never showed up. I had arranged to score 10 pieces from Pablo so that we'd score that 10 and if it went okay we'd score 20, and if that went down cool, we'd score 50. And then we wouldn't score more than 50 at any one time. We'd accumulate it in bits and pieces and there'd always be more money for them to lose than they could possibly gain by ripping us off. Plus it would be in small enough amounts that we could do it a lot faster.

But Frank stalls me for two and a half months. Finally I said, "Listen, I've got to get it on because I'm spending all my money sitting down here supporting all these people necessary to do the trip and you're doing nothing but hanging me up. You have to get down here or else. I'm going to give you two days to give me some positive evidence that you're on your way." So the next day my brother shows up from Mazatlan, bringing my dogs that I decided I wanted down there because I'd decided that the next time I went out to do anything I was going to be ready. He was bringing my dogs down and I was going to fly back and get some guns. Frank sends $1,500 with my brother to guarantee his appearance within three days.

And he never showed up!

Not only that, but he never called or in any way made any attempt to contact me, then or since then at any time whatsoever. I tried to get ahold of him at three different locations and was never able to reach him. He sent me that $1,500 and then just disappeared. Since then I've talked to a lot of people who knew Frank and *nobody* has seen him. I don't know whether he just decided to hang it up and split or he got wiped out or what. It's a complete mystery.

So with all this kind of stuff going on we were having a rough time getting it together. I mean, it's just a tough gig down there.

Chapter Eight
Success at Last

After all that mess I came back up here because I had to arrange other transportation and pick up guns and just generally get it back together again. I contacted a buddy of mine in San Francisco, Garth, who had been getting a unit ready for this kind of thing. He bought an old, heavy-duty pickup and put a camper on it, an aluminum cab, and was putting in hiding places to hold kilos. We worked out a deal. He would come down to Mexico and we'd do the thing. By this time my profit is mostly shot. Because of all the delays, by the time we get it done, the money is going to be eaten up in expenses. Plus, I have to find a driver to bring the vehicle back across. I'd never had to do that before because I'd always brought it over myself, but because I'd been busted and they knew me, I couldn't do it anymore. Garth didn't want to take the chance and Frank, my original driver, had totally disappeared.

So I had to set up a contract with a driver for five grand. That's high but I was in a jam so there was nothing else to do. Usually it's like $2500 for someone to drive the border and if it's a Mexican, it'll be 500 or a thousand and that's ideal, but it wouldn't work using that kind of a truck with American plates. Anyway, we finally line up a driver. Call him Johnny. He and Tanya are going to drive it back, looking like a vacationing American couple. He'll come down with Garth, who'll bring the truck down with the guns and another dog. So that's all lined up. I really trust Garth, he's a friend and if he says he's coming, he'll really be there. So I go back down to try to start accumulating some weed.

I'm figuring on doing it all in Acapulco, but then I decide no, I really want to know what happened with Domingo. The last time I saw him was when we were running during the ripoff. I really want to know if he was involved in that and who those people were and what it was all about and what I can do about it, because I'm still pissed. So I rent a Jeep and go back to Zihuatanejo looking for Domingo. Turns out he's staying with this American woman who runs a little lending library and cafe place where she makes lunches for people down there to sport-fish. I find out where that is and go there with a knife in my pocket, I want to know what's going on. I walk in and Domingo's sitting there drinking a Coke and when he sees me it's like he's seen a ghost.

I sit down and order a coke and he starts telling me his version of what happened. He says he ran and just kept on running. And he heard shots but he wasn't going back, he was just getting the fuck out of there. And I believe him that he didn't have anything to do with setting me up. Or let's just say I believe him, but with reservations. Mainly, I know he's got better weed at better prices if I can actually get it because I've seen sizable tastes of it, like two or three kilos, so I know it's around. So I tell him, "Look, I'm not going to score the whole amount at once. I'm going to score 10 kilos. If that goes groovy, I'll score another 20. I'm not going to have all the bread here, I'm going to score here then I'm going to put them in that Jeep and drive them to Acapulco and stash 'em someplace. Then I'll bring back more bread and get some more and take them back. You give me good weed and good weight and no bullshit and I'll buy 500 pieces. But if there's any shit at any point, that'll be it. And when we do score there's going to be a couple of us and we're going to be *on*! It won't be Grant, it'll be Garth and he's a *man*! You better be sure you line this all up straight, because if any shooting starts the first person I'll shoot is *you*." He says "No, no, it's nothing like that, I'm honest, we'll get it done right." So I say okay and Garth shows up and we rent a house in Zihuatanejo. We're going to score the first few and take them to Acapulco and if that goes right we'll score more and start bricking them up in Zihuatanejo. The house there has a back door to a hidden cellar.

So Garth and I are in Zihuatanejo and we're going to score these 10 pieces. We'll drive his camper up the road and these guys are supposed to bring the bags and load 'em in. We're both carrying big 10-inch barrel .357-magnums, state trooper specials, right out front, in our belts so everybody can see they're there. We're going to score at 11 o'clock at night off the main road. That involves driving up a really bumpy mountain dirt road, up to the top of the hill, with a guy coming down with the weed in big gunny sacks on burros. It all goes groovy, we get the 10 kilos and go back to Acapulco and start bricking them up.

Then we went back to Zihuatanejo and went out another time, spent seven hours sitting by the road waiting for these people and they didn't show up. So we go back — and I mean every time we go, we sit by the side of the road acting like there's something wrong with the truck in case anyone comes by, games like that, just standing there waiting. And they don't show up. So then the next trip they say we have to take horses and burros and meet these guys in a clearing. They're supposed to come down with the burros and weed and we're going to take a scale and weigh it and everybody's going to cover everybody. Just like the first ripoff setup. I think they were going to try to rip us off again until they realized we weren't jiving and we were ready for whatever happened.

But anyway, we take these animals and ride up into the sticks by moonlight. We leave at 7 or 8 o'clock when it gets dark and we ride until 2 in the morning and finally come to a little clearing where there's a bunch of cats with rifles huddled in the rain with plastic ponchos trying to keep the weed dry. We're sitting there with these guys waiting for the guys with the rest of the burros to deliver the rest of the weed, when suddenly a light appears off in the distance. Everybody gets real quiet and real alert because nobody really knows if it's our guys or somebody else coming through the brush. Even if it's daylight, you can't see 10 feet in the front of you the brush is so thick. At night, and raining, forget it. You hardly know if the guy standing right next to you is there. But it turns out to be our guys. We get the weed weighed and we're standing there, everybody has guns out. Domingo's got some kind of .45-caliber army pistol and Garth and I have the .357s and these other guys have rifles. We're all standing there with our guns on each other and we go through the whole trip and pay them and suddenly there's gunfire from up on the side of the hill and I'm thinking "Oh, shit, man, now what?" We start ducking and running and they fire three or four shots from up the hill. Garth fired the first shot from our side. All of a sudden I see him turn around with his gun coming up and just "BLAST!" this fucking 357 goes off like a cannon! I thought "Outasight! *Out of fucking sight!*" I turned around and we really started lacing some lead down the line, Domingo with his .45 and us with our .357s, like we're not just kidding around.

And suddenly the firing stops from the other side. It gets real quiet and we wait. It's raining. You can't hear anybody coming toward you because it's raining really hard and loud. We wait a long time and nothing happens. Finally, people start moving around and identifying themselves and it turns out that everybody, including our other contacts who'd finally opened fire on whoever was up the hill, was all there. Whoever had been shooting at us was gone and they didn't come back. I don't know to this day who they were.

So we string up our burros and horses and jump on and away we go. And we never had another minute's trouble.

Every time it was this kind of scene. We had our scoring clothes, our dark blues, dark blue shirts and sweaters, Levis, boots, bandanas. Domingo would show up and say, "Okay, it's time to go pick up another 50, be down there at 9 o'clock." It was one of those spin-the-cylinder, make sure you've got plenty of spare bullets scenes. And we got to where we were going out fairly routinely, scoring 50 pieces, bringing them back, bricking 'em up and shipping 'em to Acapulco. We finally accumulated our 500 kilos, and then ... and then we started having hassles among ourselves.

We've gotten all the stuff from Zihuatanejo to Acapulco, where we're maintaining this house in one of the better residential sections. It's a nice house, we used it again last year. It's brick construction and it's got a maid's quarters and a big, enclosed courtyard in the back and a kitchen with two refrigerators, all the modern stuff, and a dining room and living room, two bedrooms and two baths. There's a patio with a thatched roof and a pool in the front yard, a badminton court, a big lawn, really nice. At various times there were Garth and Johnny, Tanya, the driver's chick for a couple of weeks, Harry and my brother, and myself in and out of this place. Plus the camper's coming down all covered with grime and mud from the rainy-season roads, and dropping huge trunks, then being there for a couple of days and then leaving and then showing up again for a few days, so we're trying to do everything possible to make our scene look straight. When we're there we're in jet-set tropical wear, hopping around discotheques and meeting people in bars and restaurants and having people over for drinks, that sort of scene.

Meanwhile, in the back yard we've got two German shepherds and in the maid's quarters we've got the stash.

We get along really well with everyone in the neighborhood, like the kids of the woman who comes to do the laundry come over to play with the dogs, the dogs are groovy with them, as long as we're there. But the kids also know that if we aren't there and the dogs are in back, don't come near the place. So we're really digging the people and getting to be friendly with them. But we don't do anything during the day in the way of business because the maids come to bring clean sheets and the landlady stops by to make sure everything is working okay, so we never know when people may drop in. We do all our bricking at night.

We have a hydraulic press that we built out of a Snap-On wheel-puller turned upside down. It's a 20-ton press that way. We could take a kilo of weed, a full thousand grams, and compress it to 2 inches by 5 inches by 7 inches. It felt like lead when you picked one up, and it turned out it was bad for the weed, just smashed it so hard that the seeds were being crushed and the oil was getting into the weed so it tasted sort of funny. We worked inside the truck in the daytime when it was there, but I mean with everything closed, so the aluminum shell is like a reflector oven. We're in there putting in wood paneling and putting these bricks behind it and screwing the panels down and counter-sinking the screws and putting in plugs, sanding them off and then finishing it all, working in this oven in the mid-day tropical sun! And eating like horses. When Johnny and Garth and I came back north we could bend steel bars! We were really healthy.

But we started hassling. Garth was in a big hurry but I'd been doing this long enough that I wanted to make sure everything was done with meticulous attention to detail so nothing could possibly go wrong. And I've got another reason to make sure everything is really cool: Tanya is going to be riding across with Johnny to make it look like a husband-and-wife vacation scene. And Garth is just "Hurry up! Hurry up! Let's go!" So, we finally decide to go ahead. We weren't quite finished on prep work in the camper, the paneling was all in and the screws were countersunk but a lot weren't filled and big sections were unfinished and there were a lot of places where when we put the bricks in they were inconsistent in thickness, so there were bulges in the paneling that we had to try to level out by turning the screws really, really hard, then loosening others to even it out. There were some cracks between the pieces of paneling that we had to fill in so nobody could see plastic packaging reflecting from behind the paneling. The way it was done was so that as long as all that was cool, it didn't look like paneled walls, because it was a sort of stair-stepped thing so that it didn't really look like there was room to hide anything. So that work wasn't quite finished but we left Acapulco anyway and worked on the paneling as we went along. We looked sort of outrageous on the road because it was Johnny and Garth and Tanya and me plus two German shepherd dogs. Garth's hair was getting really long, so one of the other hassles was I wanted him to cut his hair because we were getting eyeballed over it. People would come up on the street and hit on us, like "Hey, *heepie*, want to buy some weed?" and stuff like that. So I wanted Garth to clean up his act but he didn't want to do it.

So finally we decide to stop at Mazatlan and finish the vehicle and make a last inspection and then I would fly back and they would drive. Garth would get out and watch the truck cross and then I would be up here to be ready to call bail bondsmen and lawyers should they get cracked at the border. Garth would keep watch down there to advise me. As soon as they got across, he was going to hitch-hike to a border crossing up at Nogales and then go up to Tucson so that if they were watching the vehicle or had any suspicion they'd all be clear of the border before anyone else bothered them.

So we get to Mazatlan and check into this motel and then this hassle started for real about Garth's hair and the way he was dressing. I said "Look, it's not going any further until the vehicle is completely finished and you clean up!" He accused me of trying to push him around and all sorts of shit and we almost got into a fistfight about it. We were working on the camper and it was the day before we were supposed to leave, and the work was pretty much completed. We had a few hours' work to do and I told him "Why don't you knock off and go get your hair cut." And it started. He says "Starting at me about the hair again, you son of a bitch?"

I said "I'm not going to get all heated up over it but we're not going anyplace until that's done."

And he said, "Well, I'll just … I'll just leave. I'll take my truck and drive it across myself."

"No, you won't, because I won't let you," I said.

"You think you can stop me?"

"Yeah, I do."

"Okay, you son of a bitch! We'll see! I'm going to get my keys!"

So he went to get his truck keys and I picked up a pipe wrench and stood in front of the door and when he came back I said "You're not going anyplace. We're doing this together and we're going to do it right. We're going to get away with it and you're not going to fuck it up. You can't make it across the border looking like you look and you know it and I know it and you're bluffing and I'm not. You try to get in this truck, I'm going to hit you with this wrench, understand? We'll get busted right here wrestling in the dirt in Mazatlan, we won't even get close to the border."

He said "You won't do it."

"Yes, I will."

Garth's a really good friend of mine so I don't know if I actually would have clubbed him but I made him believe I would, and he finally backed down and went downtown and got a haircut. But on one condition — he had to get something in, see — and at the time Tanya had really long hair and I'd been trying to get her to cut it because she was going to wear this kind of funky blonde house-wifey kind of wig crossing the border, and I had been telling her it would be safer to cut her hair because if something happened to the wig or something she didn't want to cross the border looking like a hippie. But she wouldn't go for it, and Garth had overheard some of this conversation, and one reason he wouldn't get a haircut was that she wouldn't, so his condition was that she had to get one, too. So I had her sit down and took the scissors and just chopped it off. Then I gave him 10 pesos and said, "All right, go get a haircut," and he did.

Then they left for the border and left me with my dogs and all the bricking equipment in this motel in Mazatlan. I went to the airport the next morning to fly back to get everything ready up here and I had 800 pounds of luggage. Three-hundred in *one* suitcase that was the wheel-puller we'd used, the steel box form we'd had made for the press, the pressure plate, the bottom plate, the turnscrew, the hydraulic jack, everything. So I have all that stuff plus all the hippie stuff that everybody else had been wearing and packing around, charms and god's eyes, and striped bellbottoms, all kinds of stuff like that. So I check all this in and fly into L.A.

When I come back into the country I have to register because I'm a convicted felon, and have to notify them whenever I leave and whenever I come back in. And I'm sure there's some grass in the hydraulic fluid in this jack, plus I have my dogs in traveling crates. By this time the guys in the customs office know me, so when I come in it's like "Hi, how are ya? What's shaking in your line down there?" Like they expect me to tell 'em. But I come sailing in with all this stuff and they ask to look at my luggage. I say, "Go ahead on!" And this guy starts opening stuff and goes "Aaah!" He finds a hippie style show. Then he looks at this heavy metal case and asks me to open it. He asks what it is and I tell him, and he says "Coming back in, eh?"

"Yeah, everything's done."

"Uh-huh. Okay, you can go."

I start to walk out the door and he says "By the way, you don't happen to have anything on you, in your pockets or anything?"

I say, "Nooooo."

He says, "I didn't think so," and I walk out.

Then I come back up to San Francisco and start waiting for word from the others. They're supposed to call me at a certain time, let the phone ring three times and hang up. So I get the call, which means they're going to be crossing the border at around 4 in the morning. We figured that at that time of year, sometime around the first of February, down along that border it's cold at 4 in the morning, like 20 degrees. We're crossing in Arizona and these cats are not used to being out in the cold, so we thought they wouldn't be so anxious to screw around, probably we'd get right across. So I sit waiting for further news. Checking the bail bondsmen list and pacing the floor, smoking one cigarette after another and one joint after another. About 7 in the morning I get a call from Garth in Tucson and he says "These people were supposed to be here at 6." I tell him just to wait, maybe they already came by before you got there and didn't see you and went to get coffee or something.

Then there's a long period of waiting and smoking and pacing and running over everything in my mind until the phone rings again about 11 a.m. It's Garth saying they aren't there yet. By this time I'm starting to get really worried, but I tell him "Just hang in there and see what happens." There was nothing else to do. About a long, long hour later Garth calls and says "Oh, man! They were parked in the parking lot across the street asleep!" So they were safe. About a day later these pieces were in San Francisco and it was time to unload and distribute them.

Chapter Nine
The Big Apple

To unload the camper we had to drill out the holes where the screws had been countersunk, then we had to get the screws out, they were glued in with white glue, so it wasn't easy. We needed a place to work, and there was a guy who had this place in San Francisco where he was running a few hookers and some under-the-counter watches and TVs and stuff like that, and he let us use his shop. We unloaded it and split it up so each person got his part. It was boss weed, I mean really out of sight. I got about 100 kilos and then I had to go through all the changes of selling it to get my bread out of it.

The first place I went was over to Spade Johnny's. I've known him for five or six years, we started out dealing lids and hits of acid on Haight Street. We'd stand around on the corner and rap and he'd come over to my place or I'd go to his and we'd get high and then head back down to the street to see our customers. Sometimes I bought from him and sometimes he bought from me. That's about the same as it is at this point, except instead of lids now we're doing 50 or a hundred kilos at a time. So I went over to his place and there was a cat there who was manager of one of the San Francisco rock bands who was there to score for the band. He always wants really good stuff so if you have it he'll pay top money because he works for people who can afford it. He was there and a couple of other people. They'd had some Michoacan weed, really good, that they'd been paying $150 or $175 a piece for, and I walk in and tell 'em I've got some really good weed. The rock band guy asks how much and I say two-fifty. They all say, "Ho-ho! We've got this really good Michoacan that we're not paying that much for." I tell them I think they should try my stuff before they decide. I roll up four joints, give 'em each a joint and three hours later they're all sound asleep on the floor with half a joint still in their hands. So when they get up, they're convinced, and they start pulling money out.

But there was a lot of weed in San Francisco right then, so although I was selling some at $250, it was going slow, four here, three there, five here, that kind of thing. I decided I had to go to New York because I had a few connections there, people who knew people. Besides, I felt like jamming around, taking my bread and buying some clothes and drinking and chasing some skirt, that kind of thing, because I've been down in the jungles a long time, I'm ready to party. So I load the stuff in trunks and jump a jet for New York with a list of phone numbers. I get there just after a big snowstorm that socked in the airport and I really don't know anybody directly, so I check into a hotel and start calling people. I get this cat named Dee, jump in a cab and take a kilo with me and show it to him and tell him I want $300 a kilo, just to test the waters. I'm a son of a bitch if he doesn't buy one! So I left a couple more kilos with him and I met a couple of other people and went through a lot of paranoid changes worrying about who they were and who they might be tied up with, but it turns out that one of 'em is the son of a Texas millionaire who's running around with this daughter of a very famous person, and one is a fashion magazine writer and photographer and songwriter, just an outasight cat. Then there's this Dee and his girlfriend, and I end up staying with them.

I start jamming around New York, and Janis Joplin is in town. She's staying at the Gramercy Park Hotel, and I go there to have dinner with her. We're in the bar drinking — and I mean when I say drinking, she'll leave me with my elbows sliding off the bar and jump in a cab to go to a new bar when I can't move. I can drink some, but not like her. Anyway, we're sitting at this bar at the Gramercy Park before dinner, and she's dressed in her usual style, lace hanging down her back in fifteen colors, all that stuff she wears. And when we try to go into the hotel dining room —

she's staying there, mind you, with her band and spending I'd guess $300 a day in this hotel, probably more than that — when we go to the dining room to have dinner they won't let her in because of the way she's dressed! And you'd have to know Janis, man, she's drunk and she grabs the maitre d' by the shirt front and shakes him and calls him every name in the book. "You motherfuckin' little punk! You prick!" Loud, really loud, the whole house was watching. And then checks herself and the whole band out of the hotel and moves to the Chelsea where she could dress like she wanted to, because at the Chelsea you could probably do just about anything.

So not long after that I'm having a drink with her at the Chelsea and this guy comes down who's going to Hollywood to arrange the music for some musical starring Carol Channing or Barbra Streisand or someone like that, and he tells us to come on up, he's having a going-away party because he'll be gone for a couple of months. He has the penthouse at the Chelsea — which is sort of a joke, you'd have to see the Chelsea, it's like a 3rd Street, Skid Row San Francisco hotel, only for some reason it's hip to go there even though it looks like it ought to have cockroaches. It doesn't, but it looks like it should. Anyway, this guy has the penthouse and we go up there and he's got three monkeys, a mynah bird, two parrots, two rattlesnakes, a bull snake, three piranhas, two land turtles, a small aquatic turtle, two hamsters, a whole bunch of other tropical fish, it's like a tropical zoo. There's one huge room like about 24 by 30 feet. There's a grand piano and a kingsize bed and a little alcove kitchen, a john off the kitchen, a skylight, all these plants and animals and this party with 40 people.

Among them are this black cat who earns his living being the token spade in integrated TV commercials; a few members of the cast of "Hair"; a chick who can sing like a bird and if she'd only drop about 90 pounds, she could really be big. There was a tall Swedish chick who had lived with a friend of mine on a ranch in Sonoma County three years before, maybe six-two or six-three, a beautiful woman, proportioned well but overpoweringly large. A one-man band who played piano, drums, bass and kazoo in a bar, really nice guy. Just a whole bunch of people, guys who were passing through with rock bands, different chicks, an outasight party. Over in one corner is a cat with a rock of pure crystal cocaine as big as a goose egg, shaving it down and sharing sniffs. I mean people back there are seriously sniffing some coke. I saw five guys sit around that hotel one afternoon going through an ounce of cocaine, just themselves and their friends. And two spade cats are balling some chick off in a corner, and this big Swedish chick is shooting cocaine and looking for cock, it doesn't matter who or where or when. So I thought, "Far out! I've never seen a party quite like this before." I stayed till I was too stoned to move anymore, then I split. I went back two days later and the host had gone to Hollywood but the party was still going on. Most of the same people were still there. I talked to one chick who hadn't been outside the hotel in a month. I asked her if it didn't make her claustrophobic, make her want to get outdoors and stretch her legs a bit and she said, "Naw, I don't know anybody out there. Everybody I know is right here. They live here, so there's no reason to go anyplace else."

But finally I just got so screwed up in New York … like when I got there I was used to getting up at 7 or 8 in the morning, 9 at the latest. After I'd been in New York four days, I found myself getting up at 5, 6, 7 at night! Get up when things quiet down enough to be bearable, then go out on the streets and come in at 5 or 6 in the morning to crash. That was my schedule for the two months I was there. I tried to turn it back around but it didn't happen. When I finally left, it was because I had to, I was going crazy. I'd be laying there at 4 in the morning and things would just be humming. See, you're on the fifth or sixth floor of a building and there are 27 floors above you and there are enough people moving around and making enough noise that the whole building's vibrating. And there's five or six floors below you and then the parking lots and then the subways. And airplanes flying around overhead, traffic moving all around you. It's white noise, it blows your mind and just makes you crazy. It's too much to screen out, you just can't do it. Especially after being in Mexico for a long spell. I think that's why so many people in New York are speed freaks and cocaine freaks: they have to keep their metabolism going fast enough to keep up with that fucking city. And it's a gray, ugly motherfucker, too. The streets are just cold and gray. People get totally into indoor trips there.

I met a cat there, a guy I sold some weed to, who had a beautiful, fantastic apartment, a real penthouse. This guy, a Frenchman, spends $20,000 a month on dope! Cocaine, a little taste of smack now and then, weed, I mean he buys 'em all. He doesn't sell any either, he's not a dealer, he's a consumer. He has a party and everybody has whatever they want and as much as they want. And he has a party *every* night. Blew my fucking mind, man! I mean I had guys buying five kilos at $300 apiece for their smoking stash. They weren't going to sell it to anybody, they just wanted to stay high. Some of that weed got to a U.S. senator and his wife. That's a fact. That also blew my mind. I'm sitting around smoking dope with some people and after this couple leaves, and I say "Who was that old cat and his wife?" and a guy says "That was Senator Jacob Javits," this leading Republican from New York.

One of the other San Francisco rock bands was back there and a guy I was doing business with was staying in some Texas oil millionaire's apartment who was away on some trip. A bunch of the guys from the rock band were there and they were going through cocaine like an ounce a day, smoking a lot of weed and just jamming around, going over here to get something to eat, have a few drinks, from two in the afternoon to 4 or 5 o''clock in the morning.

I'll grant you that there are a lot of great restaurants there, really good food, but you can only eat so much food and after you've been to enough parties where people are getting high and fucking all over the place you begin to wonder, if they dig each other so much why don't they go someplace private and do it? So I was ready to leave pretty quick after I got there but I was stuck, I had business to do and I had to stay till it got done.

It got to be a big drag, I started hassling with people and I finally just wrapped the thing up and came back to San Francisco.

Chapter 10
A Weird Business

After I got back to San Francisco there was this guy Johnny Frizz. He's a hippie version of the guy in Li'l Abner, Joe Btfsplk, who has this black cloud over his head everywhere he goes. Johnny even looks like the cat, sort of scruffy and drawn. He's a really nice cat, I think I met him through Grant. The first time I met him he was selling cocaine to some people from Paris who'd come all the way over here to get it, a young guy and his chick about 23, 24. Really sharply dressed, continental. They came to San Francisco to buy dope because they figured they could do a better deal here than anywhere else. That's a long way to come for cocaine! To get high? The guy must have had some long bread.

Anyway that's where I met Johnny Frizz. He had a room in San Francisco and he was dealing, but he had a run of the worst luck of anybody I've ever known. He was driving along one day — and he's maybe 5-foot-10, sort of on the skinny side, real frizzy, kinky hair, that's how he got his nickname, everybody started calling him Frizzy Johnny and then it became Johnny Frizz. His hair stuck out in real tight, frizzy bunches about eight inches around his head. And he always wore 10 pounds of beads and bells and shit like that around his neck, roach clips with deer horn on them, bells on his boots and an earring in one ear. Anyway, he was driving this old, beat-up, ripped-upholstery, black Cadillac limousine and somebody runs a red light and broadsides him. The other driver is a guy driving a brand-new Buick. He's a capital-letters Responsible Citizen in his gray flannel suit and tie and wingtips, so when the cops show up the accident is automatically Johnny's fault, no matter how it happened.

They take the other driver's information then start

hassling Johnny. They search his car, but they don't find anything, so they shake him down personally, which they have no business doing, the other car hit him and it wasn't his fault but he looks like a bust, so they search him and find a .38-caliber automatic in his pocket that he was carrying because he lived in a really rough neighborhood in the Fillmore and he's a skinny little guy so he was always getting hassled. So they're going to charge him with possession of a concealed weapon. They take his apartment keys, and it's one of those Fillmore hotel-apartment kind of trips with a key ring that has a tag with the name of the place. They take him to jail then go to his place and find a couple of hits of acid and a little bag of weed, so then they add felony drug charges. He finally gets that all dismissed, but that's the start of his run of bad luck, it wipes him out because he ends up paying over $1,200 in attorney fees and bail.

So I started fronting him stuff, a couple of kilos here and a couple of hits of acid there, and he gets things built back up to where he has about $800 in cash and he's current with me, I've just fronted him a pound of opium and he has maybe a kilo and a half of weed that he's dealing off in lids and half-pounds. But he and a friend are sitting in his apartment one night smoking hash and listening to records, just getting loaded and goofing when three guys with guns break the door down and tie Johnny and his pal in chairs in the kitchen, pistol-whip them, steal his $800 and the dope. They're in the middle of doing this when Johnny's girlfriend comes to the door and sees what's going on and Johnny hollers "Get some help!" so she runs and calls the heat. The robbers split and Johnny just manages to work himself free and untie his friend when the cops come up the stairs. He's already had a pretty heavy evening, so he shrugs and just stands there and they come in. They're there because his chick called and said some people were beating him up, and he's got this big gash on his forehead, and so on. And the cops start looking around and find a hash pipe with a little hash in it and a baggie of weed that the robbers missed, and they decide they're going to bust Johnny. Not only that, but there's this fucking pig cop who I think may be the only black narc in San Francisco and he's a motherfucker so he starts slapping Johnny and his friend around. Now Johnny's had enough and he tries to run down the stairs. The cop goes to the head of the stairs and shoots him in the leg. He's taken to the prison ward at San Francisco General Hospital. But it doesn't stop there! While he's asleep the first night there some fanatically conservative old man in the next bed tries to strangle Johnny in his sleep because he doesn't dig the way Johnny looks. Too much, man, too much! Then they move him, in his hospital gown because his clothes are all messed up with blood, to the city prison on Bryant Street. And he has to make his court appearance in this hospital gown.

He finally gets all those charges dropped somehow, at least he was that lucky, because of illegal search or he said the cats that robbed him left that dope, or whatever, I don't know. As a matter of fact, of all the cats I know who've been busted, and with some fairly substantial amounts of dope, I'm the only one who's ever done any time. Like Grant, the guy who was in that partnership with me, was busted at the San Diego airport with trunks with 150 kilos in 'em that he was trying to put on a plane. Here he is in San Diego, probably the most conservative city in California, with his hair sticking out all over his head and a mustache and beard and a roll of hundred-dollar bills in his cutoffs, and trying to ship this weed to San Francisco. Instead of checking it in through baggage, he tried to send it air freight. The guy behind the counter takes one look at him and at these trunks and calls the narcs. But he got out of it on the basis that they had no reason to open those trunks. They were padlocked shut, they had no warrant and no way of knowing what was in them and he wasn't crossing the border, they weren't customs people, so it all got thrown out of court.

But back to Johnny Frizz. He just keeps getting busted in ridiculous ways. He turned his mother on three or four years ago. Then a little later she was living in L.A. with this bar owner she'd met and Johnny goes down to visit. His mother has a little stash of weed and a little stash of acid that was hers, she hadn't gotten it from Johnny, but he had turned her on and then she started getting her own from somebody she knew in L.A. So she's married to this bar owner, he's now Johnny's stepfather. This guy doesn't know Johnny's Mom turns on, finds her stash while Johnny's staying there, assumes it's Johnny's and calls the police. Johnny and his mother come home from visiting relatives and the cops bust him for his mother's stash! So that's the kind of luck he has. It's just incredible.

But the point of all this is, when I went to Mexico year before last I left my sports car with him. When I left it was cherried out and in spotless condition, Tanya had it cherried out for me while I was in jail, and it was a beautiful car, in perfect shape, I mentioned it before. But when I got back from Mexico it was a total wreck, just ruined, totally wiped out. Unbelievable what a guy can do to a good car in that amount of time, it was mechanically and aesthetically wasted. The solid walnut frames in the seats were broken, on both the driver's and passenger's sides. How in hell he could do that, I don't know. Even if you were trying to do that, it'd be hard to do. I mean I finally just ended up pushing that car off a cliff and watching it fall and sink into the ocean. But I thought, "Well, this guy's just got bad luck."

Well, Johnny had a house in the country and a couple of dogs by this time and I had this prized German shepherd that had been with me all through Mexico and was a trained sentry dog. I spent a lot of time with that dog,

I really loved him. We were tight. I'd had him since he was a pup and he was well trained. I got him at the pound in Marin County. He was the runt of the litter and so the owners gave him to the pound. And I mean breeders would come up to me on the street and want to know his lineage. He was a prize, man! If you tried to buy a dog like him it'd probably cost you around $1500. I had him with me all through Mexico and he really helped when we went into the jungle on those trips because most people down there don't have big dogs. We had two, so when we went to talk business we'd walk in with our pistols in our belts and two huge dogs that obey you on command, people would think twice about trying to rip us off. So this dog really was my best friend.

When I went off to New York, I was still pissed at Johnny about the car, but I was in a hurry to go and Johnny had this fenced property and a couple of dogs. I didn't want to take my dog to New York, so I left him with Johnny. And son of a bitch, man, if he doesn't go into San Francisco to the Chinese New Year's celebration and take my dog. Johnny gets loaded and drunk and takes a ferris wheel ride and leaves my dog sitting at the bottom of the ferris wheel. Not tied to anything, no leash, no collar even. So of course some kids come by and toss a string of firecrackers and he splits. So the last time I ever saw him was just before I went to New York. But that's not all of it. When I had gone to Mexico I'd taken about $700 in front money from Johnny. So I get back from New York and he starts riding me about paying what I owe him. I add it all up and I say, "Look, I leave a $3500 car with you and I come back and it's a total wreck. I leave a prize dog and you lose the dog. And I already gave you three kilos, which right now I'm selling for $250 to $300 apiece. And you tell me *I* owe *you* money?"

So that's a taste of how weird it can get in the dealing trip. Some cats just don't understand what it's about. But all that went before was nothing compared with last year's trip, nothing at all.

Chapter 11
1969: Back to The Business

By the time I got through all the hassles year before last and the stress of New York, I was ready for some rest. So I and Tanya went to a little place in the country north of San Francisco. We just laid back for a while. I wasn't really thinking about going to Mexico again but after I loafed around for two or three months I started getting edgy. I had to do something pretty soon to make some bread and I was getting bored. People who knew I could score in Mexico were starting to hit on me again to make another trip. Then I came into a couple of thousand dollars unexpectedly that somebody repaid me that they'd owed me for so long I'd completely dismissed the idea I'd ever get it back. So I had some investment capital and I decided to go again.

The other thing that helped nudge me in that direction was that my father died. I'd talked to him around three weeks before that for the first time in months. He sounded really bad and then he died, and there was that whole trauma afterward that I really didn't expect. I got in touch with my brother Samuel and we went to the funeral. The scene that happened there was just a mind-blower. Neither of us had made it home for Christmas the year before that and my mother had Christmas presents for us and we had presents for them. After the funeral was arranged, we exchanged those, and my mother gave us the presents our father had bought for us. Among them was a pair of white turtleneck sweaters, one for Samuel and one for me. So we decided to wear them to the funeral under our sports jackets, which were very conservative dark colors and dark slacks and boots, black, dressy boots like we always wear. Steven had fairly long hair and a trimmed beard, but a full beard, and I had a Zapata-style mustache. All my parents' friends are pretty conservative and a lot of people on my grandfather's side of the family are right-on

John Birchers. So we're at my mother's house after the funeral and son of a bitch, man, this aunt comes up and starts in about us being so concerned about being hippies that we wouldn't show enough respect for my father to wear ties and more formal suits. There are 75 people there and she says it loud enough for everyone to hear, like she's going to put us down, right? So I decided the best way to handle was to be real direct. I yelled "Hey, bitch!" and everyone got real quiet. "The reason my brother and I wore these turtleneck sweaters is because they were Christmas presents from our father. It was a gesture of respect, understand?" Well, she could have crawled under a rock. But it was a bad scene.

Then after the funeral I had a couple of weeks of really intensively trying to keep my mother calm, helping her relocate because she didn't want to stay in the house she lived in when her husband died. Plus going through all the insurance policies and papers trying to straighten that all out and be sure she got everything taken care of, because she had never dealt with any of that, our father had done all the financial and paper work. They'd been married seven months before I was born — love child! — so there was a lot to handle. By the time I got back to the Bay Area I really wanted to get away, because it suddenly really hit me that my father was dead, and what that did to me, man — I never expected it to hit me that hard. I knew if I went to Mexico to score weed I was going to be so busy that I wouldn't have time to think about my father's death or anything else but taking care of business.

So I wrote to Domingo, or actually to this chick he was living with because he can't read Spanish let alone English. I asked if it was cool to come down. They said sure, so I started looking for transportation for the weed. After all the hassles I'd had with it the year before, I lined up three different methods for transportation this time, with people I'd known for a long time who I knew were cool.

They weren't fucking around, they weren't burning anybody, they didn't owe anyone money, they hadn't been ripped off, and they weren't dealing really heavy, so they weren't hot, and they seemed competent. They were people who had other things they did that showed they were capable of getting something done. One was a designer, one owned a store, that kind of thing. So I thought I was covered on transportation this time. I lined up a sailboat and a vehicle that were wholly owned by the people involved, so I thought I was covered. And I had plenty of bread, people wanted to invest, they'd put money in the previous year and they'd all made money. It took longer than we wanted, but it happened. So I thought, "Okay, we go."

I went to Zihuatanejo at the end of May, the end of the dry season. Everything was just uniformly brown, stubblefield brown, all the trees, the vines, everything. It was the first time I'd flown in to Zihuatanejo. Before I'd always flown to Mexico City and driven down. I flew in on a light, twin-engine, 12-passenger plane. It came in over the Sierra and flying over the top of the Sierra it's green, but when we dropped into the lowlands, it was brown everywhere. They'd been burning the stubblefields off, so it was a smell that I'd never associated with Mexico, and sort of crisp weather like autumn. It was weird because although it was fairly warm, it was cooler than I remembered it and it was dry. Always before it's been like this soggy jungle. Anyway, it was good to be back in Zihuatanejo. The cab driver remembered me, took me into town for free, we rapped about what was going on, what Americans were still around that'd been there last year and come back. There were quite a few. Some people were living on a 40-footer out near the mouth of the small bay. It was really beautiful, surrounded by hills, with a long beach and a stream emptying into the ocean, lots of coves, an arched rock to swim through. It looked like the Sonoma

County hills when they're brown at the end of summer, there was no green, even the palm trees were brown.

About two weeks after I got there I went to bed one night. It was all clear but pretty soon I'm lying there and it starts to rain. I mean, baby, it rained! I went out walking in it and the drops were as big around as your fist. They'd hit you in the hand when you held your hand out and knock your hand down! About 2 in the morning the frogs started. I'm sitting in this room with the windows open listening to the rain and all of a sudden they start up, in unison, a rhythmic thing, and within two hours the frogs were so loud I'd have to shout to make you hear me if we were as close as right now, face to face. They make this sound like "woo-woo-woo" and it starts to build up, like a gibbon whooping, but not quite that intense. Coming from everywhere, but especially down in the hollow where I guess they were hibernating until rains came. It sounded like a space ship or something.

I went across the street to this hotel where a buddy of mine was staying — he eventually ripped us off — and there was a guard sitting there because they'd had some people stealing weed and stuff, so this guy was sitting in front of the hotel with a rifle in his lap and a dog at his feet and both of them were sound asleep. I walk up and step over the dog and put my hand on the guy's shoulder and excuse myself and go into the hotel and the guy never even stirs. So I get this buddy out of bed and tell him he's got to hear this sound. He says, "What do you mean? It's 4 in the morning and I've gotta get up to listen to some sound?" I say "Listen, this is really far out!" So he gets up and comes over and on our way out the guard wakes up. I tell him there's some kind of a sound and I don't know what it is, it must be some kind of animals or something. So he jumps up like he's going to defend us, comes running over with his flashlight and his gun and kicks the dog to wake it up and we come up onto the porch. It seems to me that this sound is a way off, like maybe out at the airport maybe 2 or 3 kilometers away, right? This guard is shining his flashlight down into the yard, and finally he shines it off into the trees and says, "It's the wind in the trees." I say, "Oh, wind in the trees! That's no wind in the trees, come on!" We get in the car and start to drive out toward this sound and realize there are just millions of frogs, frogs everywhere! In your headlights down this highway there are frogs as big as coffee cans every four feet in every direction! Far fucking out!

We finally go back and go to sleep and when I look out the window in the morning, the hills are as green as an emerald, man, just shining in the sun. Fantastic! From one night's rain! Within a week it was full-on jungle, vines everywhere, something you wouldn't believe. We had a garbage pit in the back yard and five days after it started to rain, a melon plant grows out of the bottom. I had to move the garbage pit because now I had something to occupy me, a melon patch. I was a small-time melon farmer. I don't think it was three weeks afterward that there were full-size cantaloupes on that vine.

There were a lot of sailboats on the bay, two Newporter 40s, a really fine-looking 72-foot yawl, a couple of big power boats. Zihuatanejo is a fishing town. They have a big turtle fishery there, for one thing: they pack turtle sausage. They look and taste like Vienna sausage, but the turtles have meat that's almost like beef. They're big, really big, five, six feet across. They don't do anything with the shells, they just dump them out on an island where they sit and rot. If they'd just cut and polish the shell, it would be worth 20 times as much as the meat. That's been pointed out to them by a national fisheries expert but they just don't want to do that. They're fishermen, not tortoise shell cutters, they just want to harvest the meat, not cut up the shells. I saw the turtles while I was out swimming and they are beautiful.

They have a lot of sharks, too, but the funny thing is, they haven't had a recorded shark bite incident inside Zihuatanejo bay for 300 years, since some king supposedly put a charm on the bay. That's the legend, but what actually happened was this king had his people build a huge dike out of monstrous boulders after his daughter was killed by a shark. It's far out because otherwise it's just an open bay and the fishery is dumping all these fish guts that normally would attract sharks. There's a shrimp fishery there, but no sharks. Outside the bay they fish for sharks, and pack the meat and ship it to Japan. Japan is real involved in the Mexican fisheries, they've put a lot of money into boats and technicians, they built this turtle plant. Before that, the locals just caught them and ate them, up to about 10 years ago. Anyway, I've seen sharks in the 8- or 10-foot bed of a pickup, the head over the cab , the tail out over the end, dragging on the ground. A couple of guys there build dugouts, beautiful things maybe 18 feet long, out of mahogany logs, each dugout is made from one log, they're like sculptures and really solid in the water. I saw a guy paddling his canoe into the mouth of the bay sitting on top of a shark that's hanging over both sides of the boat. You tell me how that one guy by himself got that thing into the boat and I'll eat that whole fish! I don't know how he did it, it took six guys to haul it up onto the beach.

Of course, all these fishermen get stoned. Everybody thinks Mexicans don't get stoned, but these cats, man, they're stoned all the time. But almost everyone denies it, even to their friends. It's weird. I was scoring weed from this guy and he told me he didn't smoke weed. So one day I go over to his house and he's swinging in his hammock with a joint rolled in a corn husk about 12 inches long and an inch in diameter, glassy-eyed and stoned out of his mind. Not only that, but I know a father and son who go out drinking together, they go to the whorehouses together, go on trips to Acapulco and swing on the beach with the chicks and all that. They both turn on, but neither one knows that the other does. Go out somewhere with them and one of 'em'll slip off and go out and smoke a joint and come back and pretty soon the other will make some phony excuse and go off and do the same thing. It's weird, man, far out.

So anyway, the first day I got there I went to this American woman's little lending library/coffee shop on the beach. Domingo had been living with her last year and I had written before I came down. I figured they were still together. But she said no, they'd split up, he'd gone on some fantastic Mexican macho jealous trip suspecting her of being involved with some other guy. Domingo was already married and when I got there he was back living with his wife, he brought her from Agua de Correa into town and was living with her and seven or eight kids plus his sister and her six kids, and they were all living in this place about as big as a large living room in the States. So I went to see him and laid this guitar on him and things are cool, he's ready to do some business.

That same night we're standing in the street and one of his buddies runs up, a cat named Lincho with one bad eye that sort of drifts around, a skinny little kid, lazy, the laziest motherfucker you've ever seen, just won't do anything, would starve before he'd work. Wears this unbelievable bright chartreuse shirt that you can see coming for three miles. When Domingo's doing his macho trip he's sort of a hanger-on, digs hanging around with Domingo and doing little errands, delivering messages and being with him to add force to his part in the scene. He loves to be in the middle of everything and he runs up and lays this trip on Domingo about having just seen this guy Glenn, who Domingo suspects of being involved with his former girlfriend the American, over at the lunchroom hand in hand with Domingo's ex. So Domingo goes over there and gets in a fight with this woman and ends up smacking her in the face with his fist, knocking her on her can and beating her up and getting thrown in jail.

I don't think this chick and Glenn were ever really happening. Because if they were, why didn't Domingo go after Glenn? Either he couldn't handle him or he couldn't handle Glenn's action because Glenn was into heavy enough a scene that the reprisal wouldn't be worth it, so he could only vent his anger on the lady, I guess. I don't really know. Glenn's a cat I never got to know, but he's American, first of all, so he can't own land within 50 kilometers of the ocean. If you're American you can't own it, you have to have a Mexican partner. So he must have a partner because he bought land on the ocean and built a couple of palapas on it and lives down there half the year and the other half in New York, where he owns apartment buildings or something.

Anyway, now if I want to do business, first I have to bail my connection Domingo out of jail, which costs me $60. It was probably that much because the mayor wants a little and the comandante wants a little and probably the last $20 was for Domingo. The three of them probably got together and said "Here's a gringo who's got some bread, let's share some of it." Because deals with the police are just part of life down there. I knew some people who were busted in the Lake Chapala-Guadalajara area for 400 kilos, the biggest bust ever in Mexico. It was incredible, because it was in a little tiny town, San Nicolas de Ibarra, there's maybe 40 Mexicans living there, and 23 American hippies living in one house. They have psychedelic paintings all over the front of the building and they're running around with beads and bells and beards and long hair and far-out clothes and just driving up and unloading gunny sacks of weed in the courtyard of this place. I mean they're there a long time before anybody gets around to doing anything about it. They're there for *months*. Then all of a sudden I guess the Mexicans can't take it anymore so they bust 'em.

There was a special magazine supplement in the following Sunday's edition of the Mexico City newspaper about the hippies of San Nicolas. "The Cult of The Devil" they called it. With pictures of the house with incense burning in front of it, like "strange idols before Me," non-Catholic and so forth. They all eventually ended up buying their way out of it. You could say that's the rule down there. You don't get hassled when you come back to the States if you get busted down there. They make sure you get back across the border, they don't follow you around, they don't give a shit. They may have records, but down there, man, it's like "*mañana*." So you can make deals with the heat in Mexico if you have the money, but it's really hard to make a deal with the U.S. Feds, they're dedicated, they're serious about what they do, they really care. I imagine there are odd individuals who could be bought out if you had enough bread, but I don't think there are many weed smugglers with that kind of money. But in Mexico, those cats make like 20, 30 pesos a day, so a little bit of money looks like a lot.

I had taken this guitar to Domingo as a gift and the comandante sees it and loves it so I say to Domingo, "Give the comandante a nice guitar and start him wondering, start the game before he does, because we're going to be doing business here for quite a while." So we lay this about $100 guitar, a Japanese-made Aria, but a pretty good guitar, on the comandante. It's a better guitar than he's ever had his hands on so he's pretty happy, but he also wonders why I gave it to him. His name is Jorge Melindo and he's a guy who makes 20 or 30 pesos a day, which is around $2.50 U.S., for being police chief of Zihuatanejo. And I mean going to arrest anybody in that town is no joke, no easy task. An example: one of the wealthiest, most responsible and respected meat cutters in town, a butcher — and they cut their meat down there with machetes — freaked out at this town celebration and went out with his gun and shot the electrical wires for the town, blacked the town out, ruined the celebration in the *zocalo*, the town plaza, where they had decorations up and all the funky shit they put up for their parties, and this butcher shoots out the lights.

Okay, it's a night of freedom so the cops don't arrest anyone during a celebration like that. Say somebody kills somebody, they don't even bother to go after him until *mañana*, right? That's the way it is, really. In the big cities, no, but in these small villages anything can happen and everybody's got a gun. So at the celebrations they shoot off their guns all night long, they love it, it's like kids with fireworks. They'll shoot up four or five boxes of shells at a celebration. Then the next day the cops go to see this butcher at his house about shooting out the lights and he meets them at the door with a machete in hand, he's not going to any god-damned jail, no way; if it comes to it, he's going to slash and cut. But they're not taking him to jail anyway, he's a respected man, he's got some money, so they're really there to collect some money, not arrest him. If he has any sense at all he knows all he has to do is give 'em some bread. How much can it cost to buy off a cat who's only making $2.50 a day? So they finally calm him down and explain that they're just there to get some money and he pays them and they go away and everybody's happy again.

So that's the kind of scene it is, and the comandante's making a little on the side by way of presents, gifts, donations, contributions, but I also know he's a killer. The reason he got the job is he's backing the mayor's play. He's killed four men and if the mayor tells him to go kill someone else, he'll do it. So the mayor has this muscle on his side, the police chief's got a reputation as a hired gun. I figured he was going to try to get into my scene so I'd better start playing with his brain first, so we gave him the guitar.

I'd go to the whorehouse and sit around and drink

and every night the police would come and shake everybody down for weapons, then the comandante would come in and make his tour and collect dues from the chicks and dues from whoever else he happens to be collecting from, which was anybody who was doing anything illegal that he found out about. That involved probably 90 percent of the adult males in town paying him off. He'd come in and talk whatever business he happened to have, like maybe he'd have 60 kilos in his room that he wants to unload, something like that. I mean everybody in that town was selling: the comandante, the tailor, the whorehouse bartender, a dumpy 52-year-old American woman who was living there, the cat who controlled all the rentals in town, the cat who ran the discotheque.

The people who owned the biggest store in town, two brothers, identical twins — and I mean identical! I lived there four months before I realized there were two of them! — anyway, the best I could make of it after hearing the story in very rapid Spanish was that the way they got the bread to set up a grocery business was that they started out working for some sort of food distribution warehouse and they were supposed to deliver money from the warehouse each night to the boss. One night sometime between when the twin with the money left the warehouse and when he got to the delivery point, he supposedly was hit over the head, dragged into a car and taken somewhere on the coast and robbed. Actually, he and his brother got together and one slugged the other a couple of times to make it look legitimate and then they took the bread and set themselves up in a business in this little outpost they knew would be growing. And there they are today, solid citizens. How to find investment capital, right?

The richest guy in Zihuatanejo owns the building that's an Aeronaves de Mexico office, and the hotel. The telephone company office is in one of his buildings, he's got a lot going. He's a little, pot-bellied guy with a bad complexion who's nonetheless a big hit with all the chicks in town because he's got scads of bread by their accounting. And the reason he's got money is his father was an opium and marijuana smuggler. His father was in the fish business and he transported the stuff packed in fish, I'm not sure how, canned or what, but that's how he made his real money. So this rich cat has a brother who was really strung out on a lady and she broke it off for somebody else. He tried to shoot himself and missed, and just blew part of his brain away. He must've been eating opium or something. He's a pallid, sallow cat with wild mood swings. When he's up, he's laughing and giggling like something you wouldn't believe, but when he's down, he's a dragged-out walking ghost.

Anyway, all this just to say you don't understand Mexicans unless you understand that *any* way, it makes no difference how, their thing is to make some bread, more than the pittances people normally make there.

So I'd go to the whorehouse and hang out because that's where it all happens, all the action is there. The Federales' garrison is across the street, so if they have any business to do they just cross the road. The bartender's got 5 pounds of opium under the counter that he's looking to off, it's just all happening there. Nobody gets involved with the chicks, I mean you just wouldn't. You take one look at 'em, they look like a disease. Forget it! But the guys down there keep those chicks around so when they're telling a story they can reach out and grab 'em somewhere and play a mess of macho. Macho is — so far as I know it only exists in Mexico, it's a kind of Mexican men's society of one-upsmanship. A guy who's spending a lot of money and punching a lot of guys out and hanging out with a lot of groovy chicks is macho. The guy who's got the most macho is sort of the head man and can lay all this shit down and uphold a certain amount of it as truth. The macho trip started with all the rich farmers who wore all their wealth,

104

the silver and gold buttons and stuff. It was done decoratively but it was really a way of strutting your stuff right out front: "I'm a rich motherfucker, man, I'm on top of the world! I've got a boss hoss and a thousand silver coins and I'm a mean son of a bitch!" Go out on the town and drink and fight. That's what it is but they don't talk specifically about macho, you hardly ever hear the word unless somebody's putting someone else down for trying to be macho and not really making it. It's very, very primitive. All these cats are real primitive in that way.

Like the comandante is about 6 feet tall, he weighs about 200 pounds and he's a solid-looking cat. Mustache, average, well-trimmed Mexican mustache, well groomed. But he's a slimy bastard, a brute, a beast. He's potentially dangerous and I have to play a lot of games to keep him off my scene. He wears — they all wear — a flashy uniform with a flashy badge and of course his gun is always as out front as possible, he takes it out and plays with it a lot, and he's on this sort of cops-and-robbers trip. Just a brute.

The most sophisticated guy in town is the mayor, who picked up his sophistication as a pilot in the U.S. Air Force during World War II. Capitan Armando Campesino of the U.S.A.F. He ain't ever going to let go of that! I imagine he's some sort of dual citizen or was at one time. He had a plane and ran tourist flights out of Zihuatanejo to Oaxaca and and Merida and stuff like that, but then he cracked up his plane in an air show last year, sort of blew his macho there. Anyway, they decided he'd be mayor and he had some bread so he set himself up as mayor, I would guess it was his turn anyway, there are only a few cats in all those towns who run the show.

So Domingo is an Indian and the mayor is Mexican, meaning Spanish, so he's a little into this Spanish thing. All the rest of the guys are Indians. Right now 85 percent of the blood line in Mexico is Indian anyway, and out in these small towns, more so. But the comandante looks like an

Indian in a blue uniform. You look at Domingo's face and he could be Mayan, he's got the classic Indian face and he's Indian, right? But he's been into the *contrabandista* thing for a long time, it's something that's common in his family and stays in the line. It's like my grandfather used to run booze during prohibition so that's probably one way I picked up my taste for smuggling because I lived with him a lot and he was groovy. So I was around guys with names like Billy The Greek and Deacon Jones and a big spade cat called Tom Johnson who ran the whole colored trip in Portland, Oregon, for a long time. My grandfather was his bookkeeper, Tom Johnson used to bounce me on his knee. It saved my life later when I got into it with some spades and somebody happened to remember me.

But anyway, Domingo's the connection, I have to bail him out of jail. And all this happened within a week: I fly down, I'm there one day, I lay the guitar on Domingo, he gets busted, I bail him out, Tanya comes down, all in a matter of the first two or three days I'm there. It's just a typical start. Eventually I'm there five months, when I was originally only planning to be there a month. Welcome to the business.

Chapter 12
A Ripoff, Then Operation Intercept

The guy who ripped me off, did I ever run that down? He's a friend of mine, Grant, I mentioned him before, I've known him a long time, done business with him in Mexico before, like him, trust him. Some antagonisms developed between us for a lot of reasons: I lost some bread of his, he lost a camera and a bunch of valuable slides and photographs of mine. Besides, we've been through a lot of really heavy trips where the worst was allowed to show in both of us. Anyway, he came down to score and he needed my connection to do it so I set it up with Domingo. I was going to make enough money on it to mostly just take care of my own living scene until my transportation got there for this other thing I was working on.

It turns out Grant was in partnership with some other people who had recently been burned, or thought they'd been burned, by a guy named Kenny. I used to be partners with Kenny, so Grant didn't want any of his partners to know I was involved because they thought I was still working with Kenny. So I had to stay out of the picture as far as they were concerned. I figured, okay, what the hell. The bottom line is that when the time comes to score the weed from Domingo with the people Grant's working with, Grant doesn't want me there. What's supposed to happen is Grant will give a certain amount of money to the farmer to score the weed. He's supposed to put it in his truck, send the truck on its way and then come back in a car to where I am and pay Domingo and me our parts because we don't want our bread out there in the jungle and we don't want to have to carry it around there because if we do, there's a good chance it'll be stolen.

So I drop Domingo close to where things are supposed to happen, real early in the morning, and go back to the house to wait. About three hours later Domingo comes in panting, out of breath, and tells me they scored the weed, then Grant came back up the highway and dumped him out of the car and split. I had given Domingo a gun to take so if anything went wrong he'd have some protection. But the idiot loaned the gun to somebody else! Playing the Big Man, you know, "I got a big gun," and somebody sees it and says "Wow! That's great, can I borrow it?" So he goes out on this score with no weapon. When they get down the road a ways after the score, this cat pulls a gun and says, "Okay, Domingo, out of the car." At least that's the story Domingo tells me. I figure there are a lot of possibilities because I'm beginning to get to know Domingo by now. So first I tried to determine how much weed they got, which was impossible. I was told anywhere from 12 to 23 bags and everywhere from 350 kilos to 500 kilos and that they paid anywhere between 80,000 pesos and 200,000 pesos. So I know Domingo's not telling the truth. The question is, how much truth is he telling? I figure the only chance I have to find out is to catch these guys before they get out of the country.

I jump in the car and scream into Acapulco, figuring if these guys are ripping me off they're either going to drive straight out and head for Mexico City or they're going to jump on the next airplane to the United States. I get this guy I know in Acapulco and drop him off at the airport to keep an eye out for these guys because he knows them. I told him if they showed up trying to leave, fuck them up, go and say something to the customs officers, anything to hang 'em up till I get back from Mexico City. Then I head there. I figured they were driving a big, lumbering vehicle and I had a fairly fast car, an American sedan of some kind, so I race toward Mexico City figuring that if I haven't caught them by the time I get there I don't have a chance of figuring out which way they went. I don't find them, so I streak back to Acapulco and go to the airport and they haven't turned up there, so I thought they'd given me the slip. They wouldn't come and hang around Acapulco long because they'd know I was looking for them.

So I go back to Zihuatanejo and tell Tanya and Domingo I have to go back to the States to catch these guys and get my bread. I leave Domingo there with Tanya, which is when their thing started happening because I was gone a couple of weeks. After I got back to San Francisco, Grant and his people played cat and mouse games with me and I never did get my money. Finally I thought fuck it, I've got to get back to Mexico and take care of business. And now things down there got really complicated because I spent a lot of time on the beach getting hung up waiting for this and that to happen and trying to find what I wanted in the way of weed.

See, when I first got down there it was just the start of rainy season, so there was just one guy who had some weed growing. He had a waterfall on his property way up in the Sierra and he had some irrigation and it was growing but it wasn't ready yet. There was some old, pretty funky stuff left over from last season and the new stuff hadn't started to come in yet. It was the first of September before I could get any really good weed. Normally it doesn't come in till October or November. Just this guy had some in September because of his irrigation. The rain usually starts somewhere around May 1 or June and goes through June, July, August, quite a bit in September and then in September it starts to dry out. October's pretty dry, November, December and January are almost stone dry. They plant at the start of rainy season and it grows until it gets hot and dry and then they start harvesting.

You actually have to sort of deal in futures, you can calculate when it's going to be ready and what it will cost and the price varies a lot according to the season. In the middle of September some good harvests start, but most of the really good weed comes in November and December because it's planted later. It gets plenty of rain and it gets a little longer in the heat to mature. So usually between Thanksgiving and Christmas is the best time to score the top quality weed. You can still score some into January but in February it starts to thin out because there haven't been any harvests so the supply starts to peter out. There are no harvests between February and August. In past years there have been guys who stockpiled it but the demand is growing so fast in the United States and all over the world that you can't stockpile enough. I met Germans and Frenchmen and Italians and all kinds of people who were scoring. I know people who have done small quantities into the Iron Curtain countries, nothing big, but still. Mexican weed is the primo smoking product and people are coming from all over the world to get the really good varieties. People go down into the border towns to score a lid or a few lids or something like that, but people who go as far as Guadalajara or Puerto Vallarta or Merida or those kinds of places are looking to score at least 20 to 30 keys of good weed, and a lot of times more than that.

The cheapest price I've heard recently was $14 a brick out of Puerto Vallarta, but that weed isn't that good. Really good weed out of Acapulco can cost as much as $70 a piece in the off season and as little as $20 to $30 in season. The price in the U.S. doesn't vary that much because of the demand and because once you get it into the States moving it around is easy. Once it gets across the border, the really good Acapulco weed or Guerrero or Michoacan, really good Colombian or Guatemalan weed, lots of flowers, lots of pollen, sock-it-to-y' weed, you can sell for between $150 and $200 a pound and sell it fast. There are about two pounds per kilo so you can sell it for $300 to $400 a kilo really fast right now. I don't know what's going to happen this year, it seems like there's less coming in and a lot later than before. I think they scared a lot of people with Operation Intercept. I mean, it would make you hesitate, especially if you were up here and not already committed to anything. Who would go down there with that much heat on?

But we were down there already when they popped that, we had the weed lined up, we had money committed and investments made, we had to go ahead, Operation Intercept or no Operation Intercept. It cost us a lot of hassle, but the point is that Operation Intercept was a big jive. They went around pounding their chests all summer long bragging that they cut the supply off when all that really happened was that the U.S. and France and Germany and all the countries where young people were smoking weed smoked it all up. The people who usually warehoused it sold it all, they didn't have any. There was none left. The only weed that was around for us was a little that a few farmers had way up in the mountains with year-round water supplies and some irrigation that had matured at least enough that it would get you high. They could harvest that and sell it. Other than that, there wasn't any. I'm in the prime weed-growing area of Mexico and I can't score anything but shit. When I arrived, the last of the good stuff was around, there wasn't going to be any more for a while and I could only get bits and pieces. The people who ripped us off got some of the last of the good stuff and we were depending on the money we would have gotten from that to help our own business. And by the time I got back down there from chasing those cats up north, well …

So now I'm spending lots of time trying to find out who's got any, what stage it's in, how close to ready, and who the people who have it are involved with. These contacts are in various places and everybody really knows what everybody else is doing, but everybody denies it to everyone except maybe a couple of guys they're doing business with. So one of the people involved with this sort of loose syndicate that's operating in this area and that I want to do business with is who we finally come up with, which involves spending more money. That's part of the trip with the whorehouse, you go hang out where everybody's drunk and hanging out with friends to see who they're lining up with, who they're off in the corner talking with in quiet tones and so on. You pick up a little information that way but it's hard to sort it out. And then you have to figure out how to set up what you want to do. The game is either to get in and out so fast that the people who are dealing but aren't dealing directly with you don't have time to notice you, or, if you're doing an extended thing, to make them think you're doing something else, anything else. If you keep doing whatever that is long enough, eventually they'll believe that's what you're doing and forget about you. They never figured out what I was doing because I was there for so long and didn't make any moves. People came in, people left, I lounged around town, I took pictures, we weren't doing anything, we weren't bringing weed to the house, and meanwhile Domingo's running around for me. Depending on what I find out I send him someplace to check something out and he comes back with some information, or I send him somewhere to get a taste and he comes back with a taste. I'm shooting back and forth to Acapulco communicating with people who are interested in putting bread into the trip or who are supposed to be helping me arrange trips, a lot of which fell through.

Which brings up how I distinguish what I'm going to buy. First of all, you're negotiating with people about plants they have in the ground, you hardly ever negotiate with anybody over something already cut — if it's cut, it's gone. So Domingo is in touch with farmers, maybe he'll be talking to some farmer who's got a sample. He brings me the sample and I look for flowers, tops with seeds in them and small stems, and lots of growth, lots of weed and pollen, which you can tell best by looking at the seed pods. Really good grass has seed pods completely covered with pollen and then it runs out from there onto the rest of the plant. It's almost like powder. There's a real minty smell, sort of an evergreen smell when you break it up in your hands. If you break it up and slide your fingers back and forth and it feels like rosin from a pitcher's bag, and if your fingers squeak, they call it *miel*, honey. The best weed in Mexico grows at an altitude too high to be considered tropical. It grows about 7,000 feet up. I've smoked weed that was grown in the Oregon mountains that was outasight. There's an old man in Mexico I sometimes do business with just because at a certain time of year he's got fantastic weed. He's been smoking weed for 47 years, used to be a drummer and travelled around a lot, and he told me the best weed he ever smoked was grown in Denver, Colorado. The main thing is that it gets a lot of rain when it's first growing and lots of sunshine when it's maturing. Other than that, the higher it is and will still grow, it seems the better it is. The stuff that grows in Baja California, for instance, is by and large shit. It's too low there. Same with the stuff from around San Blas. Until you get up in the mountains, it's not too good. Maybe volcanic soil has something to do with it, too, because the stuff from Oregon was grown in volcanic soil, and I've heard that Maui has that soil and they get Maui Wowie, really good grass, so probably the type of soil has something to do with it, too.

Then there are the types you look for. There's one called *cola de guerro* that's also known as *sensemilla*. It has a flower about the size and shape of an egg and if you break it up there's practically no stem and a really lot of grass. It's really tight because the honey sticks it together and it forms almost a ball, the flowers stick to each other. That's another thing you look for, the stickiness. If you get a big bag of weed and it's real sticky, lots of honey on the flowers, and the seeds are real big, maybe half the size of a pea and almost black and very few seeds, maybe 10 or 15 to a whole flower, you know you're right there. There are many types of flowers. I've seen them looking like an ear of corn almost, that big around and that long. Some of those are really good, especially this sort of reddish kind. It's not Panama Red, it's more brownish, away from cinnamon toward brown, where the *cola de guerro* I'm talking about is a medium-looking green. Anyway, until you get up in the mountains, it's really not too good. The stuff that comes from Zihuatanejo is really good, but the best is grown up high.

There are mushrooms down there, too, around Zihuatanejo. Tim Leary ate mushrooms down there. There's a guy who's an ordinary farmer, who plants wheat and corn and stuff like that and a little bit of weed just to get enough extra money to buy things he needs and have a little stash for celebrations. I'd give him 100 pesos and promise him another 100 when he came through and he'd go up into the hills and pick me a shoebox full of mushrooms. They're great! They're delicious, too, we'd have them in scrambled eggs and omelets. Really fresh. We'd let them go at three days. *Hongos.* They're not illegal in Mexico and everybody knows they're hallucinogenic. And oh, man! When the farmer comes down with mushrooms he always throws in a few things that the first time I saw them I thought were just part of the mushrooms, these 12- maybe 15-inch long like stems of plants. So I looked at them and thought "Well, I'll definitely take a chance on this fluffy white mushroom, but this long black sticky thing? What is this?" And the cat just kept saying "*Amapola, amapola,* similar to marijuana, similar to *hongos*, they make you crazy in the head, they get you stoned." So I took a little bite and just barely touched the end of one with my tongue and I knew what it was — a fucking opium flower, a poppy! But just the stem of the flower with opium oozing all over it. See, the way those guys down there take opium is they take these stems and rub it off the stem on their fingers and then coat the inside of their lips with it so they're walking around licking it. It's bitter, really bitter. And it's unbelievable.

So anyway, Domingo is running around bringing in samples and I taste 'em and look at 'em and look for those black seeds. White seeds are young seeds and if they're soft and don't have the meat in them, you're dealing with a young plant. If the stuff looked too young I'd tell Domingo to tell the farmer not to cut it yet, wait till it's ripe. And then find out what he can about this farmer.

Meanwhile, I'm shooting back and forth to Acapulco communicating with people who are interested in putting money into the trip or who have bread into it or who are supposed to be helping me arrange transportation, a lot of which fell through because of the pressure on the border, because of people's paranoia or inefficiency or lack of funds and so on. I must've driven that road between Acapulco and Zihuatanejo … well, the last two or three months I was there I went every three or four days to Acapulco and back, either on the bus or driving, 235 kilometers, about a hundred miles that took about seven or eight hours because the roads are incredible. There are numerous washouts. You start at Acapulco on paved road and get about 10 miles out and all of a sudden there's a washed-out bridge and you have to drive down through this ravine that in winter is full of water from the rain. It's full. You just have to wait till it dries up after it quits raining or get towed across or something. And from there the road just gets progressively worse. There are potholes that scrape the bottoms of Jeeps, and I mean *lots* of potholes. Like, it's 30 kilometers from Zihuatanejo to Petetlan. They paved it last year, when I first got there it was paved. They put down about a quarter-inch of asphalt, no bedding or anything, so as soon as it started to rain, it started washing out. When I got there in May it was paved, you could drive 70 miles an hour on it, get from Zihuatanejo to Petetlan in half an hour. But when I left it took four hours, the road had deteriorated that much.

Anyway, so I'm driving back and forth trying to set things up. I'd get transportation set up then the guy would chicken out. Sometimes I took people up there to do something specific, rent a car or get a hotel room or something. Domingo couldn't drive, couldn't even make a phone call, had never used a phone. They got their first phone this year in Zihuatanejo, the phone company rented an office. You could go make a phone call there or wait for one to come in. But sometimes you couldn't make a call for six days at a time because every time it storms and people stop moving around there are guys who steal the copper wire. They'll steal two or three kilometers of telephone line and resell it. Then you have to wait for the company to put up new lines before you can make a phone call. I think the phone company buys it back from the thieves because it costs less than if they buy new wire.

Besides all this, there are personal things going on. There's a trip with Domingo, who is, first of all, a typical Indian-Mexican, small-village, backwoods, jungle weed connection kind of a cat. He was born in a place called Agua de Correa, only about 200 people. A *correa* is a leather strap, and *agua de correa*, "water of leather strap," refers back to how the place was named. There was a guy who carried mail before there were any roads in the area, who knows how long ago, it might have been before the *conquistadores* got there. This guy carried mail or messages along this trail and he stopped to wash his feet in a stream and took off his sandals and the straps for his sandals. One strap got away and floated downstream and ended up in a woman's water jug. So that's where the town got its name, water of the leather strap. To this day it's a very primitive place. They are actually Indians there and they've been there for hundreds of years. Some of them speak Spanish now, some don't. So Domingo's a primitive cat, right? He grew up climbing coconut trees like an iguana, cutting through the jungle with a machete, things like that. In terms of civilization, he's a ding-a-ling, a complete incompetent, but he grew up running around these hills and he knows good weed.

So he gets into the weed business and starts out selling lids on the beach. When I met him he was doing that and working at the palapa for us. So by selling weed, he suddenly has three or four hundred pesos and he's never had more than that at a time, it's like 40 or 50 U.S. dollars. I come down there and I've got lots of bread to spend, right? But he's the kind of guy that I could lay $600 on him to do some business and he could spend all that money in that town within 24 hours and not buy anything, have nothing to show for it, just spend the money. And when I say he can do that, it's because I've seen him do it! I gave him 600 bucks to give this other guy so much to do this part of a deal and to pay another guy so much to do another part of the deal. I gave it to him at 7 o'clock one night — and all the stores close at 8, right? — and he came back the next afternoon and nobody had gotten the money they were supposed to and Domingo was stone fucking broke. Not only that, but he hasn't bought anything. He hasn't bought a pair of shoes or anything. Who knows how he did it? I couldn't spend $600 in this town in 24 hours and not buy anything. I wouldn't know how to go about it. But Domingo knows how. He wasn't buying anything, he had the bread in his hand and he went out and spent all the bread. He probably went to the cathouse and bought everybody a beer and bought a couple of rounds with the chicks and maybe rode around in taxicabs all night, who knows? He spent the money. He's the kind of a cat who if he has $30,000 in his hands he'll spend every penny within two months and have nothing to show for it.

When I left after the trip before this one, he had two pistols that I'd given him, he had a guitar, a transistor radio, a couple of wristwatches, and a few thousand dollars. And a bunch of odds and ends that you might think someone would hang onto, like a good Hohner Echo harp, a harmonica, and other little musical instruments that he liked to play. And when I went back in May, five months later, he didn't have any of these things. Not even the little music instruments. He was into a trip where he would spend money until it was all gone and until there was no possible way he could spend more.

So I had that personality to deal with, but the fact remains that he can get the best possible weed, he knows how to go about setting the trip up. He's been doing it long enough that he's gotten the idea how it works. Plus he's got a real, almost subconscious cunning. A lot of times it's working and he's not even aware of it, it's just his natural way of behaving. If you were to ask him about it, he'd be insulted because he believes he is honest, that he never lies, doesn't cheat, doesn't steal. He can be walking out of the house stealing a knife from you and at the same time believe that he is a straight-shooter, because he is a macho cat, and that's part of that mentality that's just really far out. He can lie to you with a straight face and be sincere, because when he puts himself on the trip of being a righteous cat, he believes that's what he's going to do: he's going to be honest and righteous and not devious. But it's not possible for him to do that, his nature and training is otherwise.

And oh, man! So many people get involved in it. I get involved with two old ladies, right? I have a lot of friends who're on this three-pillow bed trip so it seems appetizing. Seems like it would work, it wouldn't be too hard. I already have Tanya, she's been my wife for seven years. Seven-year itch, I guess. See, I had to make that trip back north because of the guy who ripped me off, and I met Sally, this pretty chick up there, through a friend, and Tanya and I had talked about the possibility of sometime having another lady in the house. I was attracted to this chick, and I realize Tanya is beginning to drift away so I think maybe another chick will get her attention. Plus I'm on a funny trip, I'm on a Capricorn business trip and it's not coming down right, so I'm penned into all kinds of frustration. Because of that, I'm not paying much attention to Tanya. So I suddenly notice her and Domingo holding hands and shit like that, and I face both of them down with it and they deny it. But I'm trying to keep the business trip going, so I hope it's not anything serious and that if I let them go ahead maybe it'll all work out and I can avoid any trouble that'll fuck up the business trip.

So I'm eating a lot of crow because of Domingo because he freaks out easy and every time he freaks out I have to be real nice and soothing, otherwise it could blow a lot of business that I've worked real hard for. So when he goes on one of his trips about how he's going to blow my whole scene and do this and do that, instead of doing what I'm normally inclined to do when somebody's laying shit like that on me, I just stay diplomatic. But I'm not digging it. And all of a sudden I have this opportunity to have two pretty chicks in the house and really hit Domingo right smack on the button with macho. I just can't resist all these temptations rolled into one, so I bring this chick down to Mexico and put together a three-pillow bed and proceed to play macho. It was all out front, I talked to both of the ladies about it and they understood the circumstances or at least said they did. It was really groovy for a while, for "FLASH!" an instant in time, it was paradise. Or at least I thought everybody was grooving with it for while, but I'm not so sure now. Anyway, it was only a flash and then it began to become obvious to all parties that it wasn't going to work. And it didn't. And that ain't saying nothing! It's too much pain, man, I'd just as soon this'd be happier. But anyway …

Then I got sick. And I got sicker and sicker. Tropical disease, dysentery is rampant, there's little red worms in the drinking water. I mean, I hated to shower there because I knew I was getting these worms on me. You pour the water out of the tap into a bowl and you can see them swimming around. Incredible! They pump the water out of the swamp. So my body is debilitating, and I don't really have the strength to play macho. What I really want to do is just rest. Get some peace and quiet. But by then it's on a real personal trip that gets real involved because Tanya's real interested in Domingo, who by this time I really don't dig, because he knows me and he's got me in a place where I have to count on him and he's really rubbing it in. Plus he's digging Tanya and trying to pull her away from me because he can't stand me having two chicks.

And by this time Samuel is freaking out. My brother came down somewhere in the middle of all this to try to help with the business trip and he's real protective of me, so when he starts to see what's happening between Domingo and Tanya, he starts getting into a lot of friction with them. I realize that all this is happening so I'm trying to get my strength back to be my light, gay, charming self. But I can't even really think. I'm so sick with all this shit oozing out of my pores that to think anything through to a decision is … I'm a fevered brain, right? I've got tropical fevers in my system and to try to think is just, sweat pours.

So I finally realize that what I have to do is spend more time with Tanya, who I really dig, if I'm going to keep her. And get my health back so I can handle both of them, if that's what's going to happen. Or at least get strong enough to handle the situation of somehow easing out this other chick if it's not going to work. What I'm really interested in doing is getting Tanya back. So I slowly get my strength up and spend some time at the beach and start to get a tan, and I'm running again and playing with the dog, the big German shepherd we brought down to keep people away from the place, and I'm eating right and I decide I'd better take the ladies out drinking and dancing and we'll get drunk and get loaded and have a good time and everybody'll relax and see that I'm capable of being my old charming self.

Then one day I'm running on the beach with the dog and I step in a crab hole and break two toes. That night I'm supposed to take them dancing. They have their frocks all ironed, I have my pants pressed, ready to go and I break two toes, man, just bigger than shit. Plus, I still have to go through all the running around in the jungle now because the business has been set up, it's going to happen, and I've got two broken toes. If you've ever walked on some of those fucking trails, this is no joke. I can't get a cast or I won't be able to handle it at all. I can only walk on my heel, I have to go out in the jungle to inspect a load of weed, I'm picking up 40 pieces, and I have to do it on a pair of broken toes. That involves driving 42 miles on a rough road because Domingo can't drive. The one time I let him drive a car was when I was so god-damned tired from driving back and forth that I let him drive so I could rest, and he drove us into the middle of a river. So what can I do, take one of the chicks out there with me carrying a .45 or something?

So I drove and walked miles up the sides of mountains with those broken toes. There was nothing else I could do, I had to get there.

Chapter 13
Operation Revenge

Meanwhile people are bombing out all this time because they don't have any bread, people get busted, all kinds of hangups. So things stretch out and all along Domingo keeps wanting money and if he doesn't get it he hangs around and sulks and makes scenes and says he's going to drop the whole thing, he's going to get a job, "I'm going back to fishing for a living," which is a crock of shit but I have to play all these funny little games with him, plus I have to keep at least enough cash coming to keep his mouth shut, so I'm consistently running out of money and having to find more so I can wait some more. That means looking for somebody who's stout enough to put cash into a Mexico trip.

For a long time most of the hassles that hung us up weren't Domingo's fault, there were other things. Sometimes it was because he wasn't doing something or because he was doing the best he could but he couldn't accomplish what we needed, so it took a long time to finally get things together. I finally ended up with backers on the East and West Coast and in the Midwest all waiting for results. It wasn't a big co-op or anything like that, it was just that I would happen to know someone somewhere who was in the business so I'd get a grand here and a grand there. That's just the way it worked as we went along. I went down with my own money to begin with, then people kept coming down to do business. I didn't want all these people involved but after the ripoff we had so much invested that I couldn't afford to drop it. It seemed like it was likely to get better pretty soon. So I would contact someone and they'd come down and look it over. Some would leave some bread and some wouldn't. Some would say "No, thanks, I'm not interested in getting into that

122

insane trip." And there were a lot of things that just wouldn't happen. Guys would think from north of the border that they'd come down and pick up a hundred pieces and shoot back up north, but they'd get down here and see all the flashing lights and people in uniforms at the border for Operation Intercept, and they'd see cats carrying machetes along the roads, and they'd decide they just wanted to go home and rest. People just chickened out.

Operation Intercept popped up right in the middle of our trip. We were still in Zihuatanejo setting things up. They sprang it right at the wrong time for me because it was getting close to when I was supposed to pick up this weed. I'd gone through a long process of finding where to do it and setting it all up and I was having to put investors off about the bread. The transportation was ready to go just when Operation Intercept began and then the transportation people all said, "Oh, no, baby, I'm not going." So Operation Intercept cost me a whole lot of time and a whole lot of pressure and more trouble. They'd talked about cracking down but they'd never talked about the kind of grand-scale border stoppage that they went into. That was a total surprise. I mean they caught people in line at the border who just happened to be there when it started and couldn't get out of line. They stopped more than 500,000 vehicles the first day! They got some people, they got 200 kilos in one place and 200 in another place because people were in transit and didn't hear about the crackdown. There may have been a lot of advance information up north but I'd been down there a tremendously long time, too long to hear about it. I was in Guerrero and you couldn't even buy an English-language newspaper in Zihuatanejo. I'd been there for months so I never heard it was coming.

And that wasn't all they did, the Mexican government went on a spraying trip. Everybody claimed it was a defoliant they were using on marijuana crops, but it wasn't, it was a nauseant! They definitely were using it because I had some of that grass. When you smoked it, it made you nauseous. When we were in Phoenix we got some grass that smelled and looked funny. We didn't pay much attention to it, we rolled some up, about six of us, and smoked a bunch of it and got a little high, but not very much, and all of a sudden I realized I was just vaguely nauseous. And it increased. The more grass I smoked, the worse it got. So I thought, "This is shitty weed, I won't smoke any more of it, it seems to be making me sick." So I put it down and it wasn't until about a week later that the same bunch of us were together and we started talking about that weed and found out that every one of us had gotten sick. About a week later some more came in from somebody else. It had the same taste and did the same thing, it made a couple of chicks throw up right away. But it wasn't as strong as they said it was going to be. They said it would cause uncontrollable vomiting instantaneously. It made me feel woozy and nauseated, but I never did throw up. Those two chicks really lost it though.

So anyway, just when I had a guy with a boat who was set to load and bring the weed back, all of a sudden they pop Operation Intercept. There are radar boats and helicopters all over the place 24 hours a day and they're ripping everything to bits at the border and my boat transportation guy says, "Oh, no, that boat's my lady, that's my life, that's all my bread, I can't do it."

Now understand that besides this, the people in Guerrero form factions. Usually the weed farmer's whole family is involved. They're way off in the sticks someplace and protecting the stuff. When they get ready to sell, a couple of things can happen: they can try to sell it without the Federales' help and run the risk of getting caught, possibly in a gunfight, and all the other hassles involved with that; or they can try to deal through the Federales and, yes, take essentially the same chances. They're just as likely to get ripped off if they're trying to do business with the Federales as if they're trying to avoid them. So I really don't know how this deal worked, whether the Federales were actually working with the farmer from the beginning or whether they caught him with the weed and are going to have him sell it and take a piece of the action while protecting it to make sure it happens. But we finally found out through a group of people who acted as liaisons between the Federales and the farmers that they were involved with this farmer who was supposed to have all this weed. We had an offer from a guy and found out he was linked with the people who'd ripped us off the year before. So we decided this was our chance to get back at 'em. So I'm putting this information together so I can rip off these guys for taking me off the year before. I know they've got a whole bunch of weed and I know they have different people taking care of it and fronting it for them. At one point before they approached us to buy we found out where the field was and we were just going to rip it off. We decided we would just wait until it was ripe and then go pick it when they weren't around. We had it all planned, had burros and horses all lined up. There were no roads out there, we would have had to take horses and burros up there to look around in the daytime and then load the stuff at night and split. But then we were approached by somebody who was working with these people and with the heat to buy this weed. We knew it was the same people that ripped us off before, but they didn't know we knew. So we agreed to buy 40 kilos to see if they did have the weed, to see what it looked like, and whether we wanted to bother with more if it came down the way it should come down and to see how the people who were sitting on the weed for us in Acapulco would react. In other words, just to test the whole thing out and fine-tune it if it needed tuning. And it turned out it needed a *whole lot* of tuning.

About the middle of September when the stuff finally got ripe enough to pick we arranged to meet this guy to get the weed about 5 miles off the main road that comes north from Acapulco and about 45 miles toward Acapulco from Zihuatanejo. We go and meet these guys and we don't know what's going to happen. They know we're coming to get it and the only reason we're willing to do that is that we're negotiating to buy a much larger amount involving a lot more money but we want to start with a smaller quantity to see if the weed is worth messing around with and if it looks like it's actually going to be possible to do what we want to do, to get even for last year.

So we get down there and take our walk off through the jungle — and you know, there's really nothing in this world quite like going off into the jungle with a Mexican Indian who's chasing your old lady behind your back and you know it and you've faced him with it and he's denied it, and *he's* supposed be backing you up if anything happens — dig it? I figured I was just as likely to get shot by Domingo as anyone else, probably more likely. But we take our walk through the jungle by moonlight, me with my broken toes. And we pick these bags up and pay these people and take 'em back and take them to Acapulco where we had the other rented place to stash it. All that goes all right, but then on the way back to Zihuatanejo to arrange to pick up the rest of it, the large quantity, Domingo drives us into the river. I wake up and there's water coming over the windowsills of the car. If you opened the door, the thing would have … I don't know, Domingo started to open the door and I said "Hey, man, don't do that! This thing'll probably hold the water out but if you open the door, we'll have a river running through our laps." So we crawled out the windows and got back to shore. We're sitting there waiting for it to get light so we can see what to do, because the car won't start, it's filled and the engine's submerged. I mean he was driving about 60 miles an hour and the bridge was washed out and he just drove into it. Fortunately, it had a grade that was fairly gradual, it wasn't like going off a

126

cliff.

So we're sitting there and this big vehicle drives up and starts across. All of a sudden I realize it's two Americans speaking English. They're in a huge camper, I mean a $10,000 camper, I don't know what kind but I've seen them before, the perfect vehicle for smuggling. A couple of cats who look rich and this Swedish-built or something like that, all one piece like an Airstream trailer, only more aerodynamic. Inside was a lot of teakwood, natural fibers, it was a beautiful thing! It's 4 in the morning and they're really gettin' it on, wading in the river to see how deep it is and so forth, and I think to myself "There's only one reason why a couple of Americans would be crossing the river at 4 a.m.: they can't wait for dawn to see what they can do with the river crossing, they have to make it across *now*, they've got a load on!"

And I mean these guys were so cool. They got across the river, stopped the camper, got out, stretched, went around to the back door to get a drink of water and a glass of orange juice, smoked a cigarette, then got back in their camper and went on their way. It turns out that they had two tons of weed stacked in this camper and were working with this big macho weed dealer the Federales were looking for, a kind of Guerrero mountain bandit who flaunts it. He'll come into town with two swift-looking chicks — he's about 50 and has a son who's 25 — and he's always got three or four other guys with him and they'll come rolling into town roaring drunk, shooting off their guns, kicking places apart, just raising hell. Then he'll go back into the mountains and say, "Okay, motherfuckers, you want me, come and get me." And they won't go. Because they sent 23 Federales after these guys about a year and a half ago and they got about eight miles off the main highway between Acapulco and Zihuatanejo and 18 of them were dead. The ones who got back never even saw the people who shot them. I mean, when people talk about

Guerrero *bandidos*, they're not jiving, these cats are *bad*. And the Federales are no angels either, I told you about them ripping us off the trip before this one.

I don't know if the guys with the camper made it across the border but I haven't heard of any two-ton busts. They looked like the kind of cats who would make it. One was wearing amber shooting glasses, they were young, groovy-looking cats who made me think when I talked with them for a while that they would make it. They were smooth, very nice cats, friendly. We didn't ask them for help because they obviously had other business to take care of, they already had their load on and we were still just setting ours up, so I didn't even ask them. Why spoil a good act like they had going? Domingo and I waited till it got light, then pushed the car out of the river, me with my fucking broken toes. We pushed it out and got it started and went back to Zihuatanejo.

Then there was about two weeks between the first 40 pieces and the 680 kilos we ripped off the Federales. We got the 40 and took them to Acapulco and sat on them for a couple of days to take a look around and see that we weren't being followed or watched, that they weren't making any attempts to locate us. See, I sent this guy who was down there as a watchdog for some people who had money in the trip and my brother Samuel and another guy who was down to help us with transportation, I sent them into Acapulco to rent a place and then Domingo and I and the two chicks stayed in Zihuatanejo. So then we told 'em yes, we would take the rest of the weed but it was too much to carry back to the car. The 40 kilos weighed about 90 pounds, so Domingo and I each carried about 45 pounds, but how the fuck are we going to get 680 kilos out of the jungle? We had to wait for the roads to dry out so we could use a vehicle. We almost blew it. Rain started about the time we left Acapulco to go north to do the 680. By the time we got there, the roads were slipping and sliding. And that delay was because from the very beginning, for one reason and another, people were finking out. Three days before we were supposed to do the pick-up I had a vehicle. It was there. But then the driver got paranoid and split and left me with no transportation. I was in Zihuatanejo one day and he came up and told me and drove away. I haven't seen him since. Not just because of Operation Intercept, he'd been there waiting for a week for the go-ahead and he was really on edge. So I just kept getting hung up and hung up and hung up.

Part of it was just the time it took to get information and sort it all out. The cat we were working through claimed to be a farmer. Whether he really was, I don't know. His name was Luis, he might've been a farmer or he might have been one of these — see, it's really hard to know who you're dealing with because there are bandits running around dressed like Federales just to rip people off and lay it on the Federales. And there are Federales running around dressed up like anybody else trying to find out what's going on so *they* can rip somebody off. It's crazy. And there are American law enforcement agencies paying people to work for them. So it takes a long time to find out where anybody's really at and even then you're never really sure.

I didn't originally go down there to rip anybody off, I went to do that other business that ended up with not getting the money. So we began considering other options after we lost out on the first one. We'd expected to make enough money on the first deal to move a shipment of our own and come out ahead. Then we started getting rumors about the alliances that had formed involving people who'd ripped us off the year before. We didn't really hurt them. They had like 40 tons of weed and we got 680 kilos. And we evened up an old score. Opportunity presented itself and it got to the point where we didn't have anywhere near the bread to do what we wanted to do, so we didn't expect to be into this big a quantity. We were originally going to move a couple of hundred pieces of our own but all of a sudden we had the opportunity of getting six or seven hundred, so we took it. And rip-offs are just a hazard of the profession.

You have to figure if you go down, especially if you go as far as Guerrero or Yucatan or Oaxaca or anywhere like that, people don't even have a pair of shoes. They grow tomatoes and if they have any left that they don't eat or preserve, they're selling 'em for 4 pesos a kilo and they only get somewhere between a few kilos and maybe 500 kilos a year to sell, depending on their crops. The average, overall Mexican income is less than $500 U.S. a year. You have to figure that if that's the average, what's an Indian 50 miles from the nearest paved road going to make? He's not making anything, I mean, really nothing, zero. Some of them never see cash. There are tribes living in the Guerrero hills that don't even wear clothes. Nothing. Ever. They don't speak Spanish, there's no one within 20 miles of them who speaks Spanish. And even if there were, they couldn't get to them because the jungle's so thick and the cliffs are so steep. They're still living in the fucking Stone Age. Then somebody lets them know that if they cut some of the weed that's growing around there they can sell it and get a lot of stuff they might like to have. All of a sudden they're into a business where they get a kilo of something and it's worth anywhere from 40 pesos at a low to maybe 300 pesos at a high. So you're talking about tens of thousands of dollars in American money. That's a big enough temptation to people in the United States who see lots of money all the time, but to these cats, man! Five grand, 10 grand? Whoo! That's a stack of loot! So there are a lot of rip-offs. When I went down last year I carried about 10 grand in front and ended up getting ripped off for about $2,500, which meant I had to make up other people's portions of the money out of my part of the profit. So I just broke even. When I got back home, I had enough money to straighten everybody out and pay bills that were due and keep everything current, and just enough left to live on for a while.

Anyway, when we're ready to pick up the 680 kilos, we're supposed to meet them someplace we can drive a vehicle, which means going off the main highway up this road into the Sierra Madre. We had to put it off about 10 days because of road conditions, we had to wait until we had about three days with no rain so the road would be dry enough. They were going to have the weed there, expecting us to pick it up and pay them but we were ripping them off, one way or another. We set it up so that the cats who were actually in charge of their operation would be waiting in a house in Zihuatanejo. It still had what they assumed was all our personal belongings in it. We told them we weren't bringing the money for that many kilos out to the jungle because they might just rip us off. We said we'd come out there, load the weed, the truck would take off and we'd maintain communications with it. For all they knew we had radio-telephones, we let them think we had walkie-talkies to stay in touch with the people in the truck. They've seen the CIA there with that kind of equipment and we seem to have more bread than the CIA, or at least they've seen more of it, so to them, we could easily have that kind of gear. When I finally got all this stuff into Acapulco, I went to Sanborn's and ran into the American chick that the comandante was running around with. I introduced her to some friends of mine and went to go make some phone calls and while they were having a drink she told them how cool she thought it was to be running around with me because she and her friends thought I was CIA. She said I'd lived so long in Zihuatanejo and been hanging out at the whorehouse and in and out of everybody's scene but hadn't done anything, and I'd had people come down and look around town for a couple of days and then leave, so people

131

had decided I was CIA.

So the people we're dealing with believe we have that kind of equipment and we tell them that as soon as the truck is safely beyond a certain point where they can't possibly know what's happening with it — for all they know we've been changing trucks, they're thinking we're a big, sophisticated operation, and they're going for it, they're eating it up. We tell them as soon as we find out the truck is safe, we'll go back to Zihuatanejo to what they think is my house, where we'd had business conversations with them, and pay them. There's an expensive stereo and clothes and all kinds of stuff there and a Jeep parked in front, so it looks like I wouldn't just leave everything there, there's no chance I'd split and leave all that stuff there. But I can afford to do that and still make out like a bandit. And bandit is *exactly* on it! Whoo! And they deserved it, but they'd sure like to get ahold of us now. From what I hear, they really searched for us. I never went back to that house. But I have to straighten things out with the rent-a-car people if I go back. I wrote a letter and told them where the Jeep was. I imagine it was missing a few parts by the time they got it back, if they got it back.

But it ended up that when the time came to make the pickup, we had no vehicle because of the guy who split. We had to pick the stuff up one way or another. I mean, if we had to rent five cars to do it, that's what we would do. But my brother had met these hippies in Acapulco who had a beat-up VW bus that they were running around Mexico in. They said they'd rent it to us for $100. So we rented it and went to pick the weed up. And we got up there and just *stuffed* the bus until we couldn't get any more in. We loaded eight big gunny sacks on top and tied them down and we packed about, I don't know, maybe 25 bags inside. The middle and back seats were out and these bags were so tight there was barely room for Samuel to drive, it was stacked up right next to him. They had three times as much weed there as we managed to get into the bus, if we had a bigger vehicle we could have taken it all.

But we didn't know beforehand exactly how it was all going to go down, whether they would try to rip us off or what. There must have been 20 Federales standing there with machine guns and automatic rifles and pistols and machetes. It was hard to tell how many there were because they were running around bringing the weed out, it was pretty well concealed about 200 yards off in the brush. It's the rainy season, so if you're off in the brush and two feet away from an elephant, you wouldn't be able to see it. If you have a house out there and go away for a week, when you come back you're going to have to cut your trail through with a machete, because it's grown over. So we finish loading and get in our respective vehicles and drive away, wondering if they'll start shooting, if we'll have to shoot back, they might chase us, they might do anything. But it comes down that we load the bus, tie it all down, jump in and drive away and they just stand there and watch. *"Muchas gracias, senores, hasta luego!"* Later! And at the highway, instead of turning north to Zihuatanejo, we turn south toward Acapulco.

So Samuel is driving the VW bus covered with a tarp flapping in the wind. Goofy Gus, who came down to help, is driving the beast I have now, the Kharman Ghia. They call him Goofy for a reason. He's a real freako. So he's driving that and I'm in some kind of American sedan I rented because I wanted something dependable. Domingo's riding with me. Gus is staying close to the bus, a little ahead, a little behind, just in case anything happens because the wheels on the Ghia are interchangeable with the ones on the bus and there's no spare on the van. When we got about half an hour away from the people we ripped off, I stopped and just waited to be sure nobody was following us. We wait about 15 minutes, then take off again. That way I could sweep up from behind if they got into any kind of hassle, I could come up out of nowhere and see if I could do something, whatever was necessary.

And weird shit always happens in Mexico. We're driving around this long, long curve and over on the left side of the road there's a car parked and two guys and a chick outside the car. Something funny's going on, this guy's shooting a gun, it's something weird. But we're following this load we've got on so whatever's happening, we're not stopping. We go shooting by and it's this mountain bandit I mentioned before, it's him and his son, they're obviously both drunk and they're making this chick dance by shooting at the ground by her feet and she's like *terrified.* We come around this curve and see this in the headlights of our car and just "Tsshhht-poom!" go right past into the darkness. Just thinking "Far out!" Surrealistic.

Then we're going along and we don't come up on our people for a long time, so we figure everything's cool. We get to this place where the river had washed out the road,. there's water running across the road, and it varies in depth. I mean road repair there is, the road washes away and they throw in some sand and it washes away again and they throw in more sand, and that's road repair. So sometimes the water is 12 inches deep to 2 feet deep and if you take it real slow you can make it. But sometimes it's 4 feet deep and you get out in the middle and there's no chance. So we don't know what's going to happen. There's a family living about half a mile off the road, about 30 or 40 people, including 10 men anywhere from 16 to 50 living in the house, so if you get stuck in this river you can, if you have a flashlight and if you don't mind walking into the middle of the Guerrero jungle at night, you can wake these people up and they'll come and push and pull your car across. When we get to the river, we see no sign of our people, so we figure they must have made it, it must be cool, so we cross the river, it's cool, and then we sit back and relax and start to rap.

134

We're skimming down the highway and we come into a little town maybe a hundred miles out of Acapulco and over on the right side of the road is one bright red Volkswagen bus, and one bright red Karman Ghia parked in front of it. The engine compartment at the back of the bus is open and there are tools on the ground and I see my brother, sweating, wild-eyed. I can see Gus hunched over the engine cursing and swearing and trying to clean the points. Ooooh, man … But finally he gets it back together. By this time it's sunrise. We had calculated everything to be stashed at the house in Acapulco by sunrise, but we're late, the sun is coming up, people are starting to move around now because people down there get up early. People are wandering up and down the road, waiting for rides, going to their potato fields or their corn fields or whatever they have happening. Trucks are going up and down the road and cops every once in a while, and here's this VW sitting there with these eight bulges on the roofline and tarps hanging over. I mean if you get close to the van, you can smell the weed. And the Mexicans, of course the last thing they're going to do is turn you in to the heat, not that they care about you, they just want no hassles with the heat. But they know what's happening, they come over and look around, walk around the van and look at you and say to themselves "O-ho! Far out!"

So we need some rope. We don't have any more rope, all the rope we have is holding the weed on the roof, so there's nothing to tow with. I take the car and shoot about 10 miles up the road at fucking breakneck speed, barely missing cows, I'm sure there was hair on the bumpers. I ask somebody in the next town where I can buy some rope. The cat points up the street so I pull up in front of this place and jump out, run inside, yell for the woman, trying to hurry, and the woman … slowly … walks … out.

I blurt "Iwannabuysomerope!"

She says, "Well, what kind of rope would you like?

We have this kind and we have that kind and—"

"Just gimme some good, strong rope, that one's good!"

She takes the rope out.

She starts to weigh it out.

She asks how much I want.

"You sell it by weight, right?"

"Kilos, senor, by kilos."

So I say "Give me 50 pesos worth, I don't care, just a good long, heavy rope!"

So she slowly starts to put rope on the scales. She weighs it out to 50 pesos worth a coil at a time. Puts a little on, takes a little off to make sure it's just right. And I'm thinking "God! Fuck this!" My brother's sitting back there freaking out and the heat is starting to patrol around, I've seen a Federale patrol on the road already heading in our direction and I'm thinking "AAAGH! Come on! Gimme the god-damn rope!"

Finally I just throw the money on the counter, grab the knife, cut the rope, throw it in the car and streak back to the bus. We rope the van behind the rent-a-car and tow it up the road with Gus and Domingo in the Ghia, because since I'm towing the weed now, Domingo doesn't want to ride with me anymore, he's afraid we're going to be busted. I was afraid, too, but it was my brother in the bus, right? And he was going to sit on that weed till it was safe or it was busted, there was no way I could talk him into just pushing this load off a cliff and forgetting the whole trip. If you knew Samuel, you'd know there's no way to change his approach to anything once he's made his mind up. So I had to tow him.

So then I have Gus shoot up ahead to check the road out and come back and tell us if he finds anything dangerous, if the fiscal checkpoint is open, if they're stopping cars, if there are any masses of Federales on the road, anything like that. I'll just hang behind. The only problem is that even towing the van I can go faster than he can in that beat-out Ghia. So I'm constantly running up behind him and having to slow down, but I don't want to slow down, man, I want to steam on through, I don't want to be towing this thing any longer than I have to. Driving that van down the road was bad enough, but towing it? It's just too much. One gringo in his big, brand-new rent-a-car towing a crummy, cruddy-looking VW bus loaded to the gills? *Ooooo*-kay.

First we get to Pie de la Cuesta, where there's a Federal checkpoint, a fiscal stop where they shake down truckers mostly. There's a garrison right behind this checkpoint, so there's a bunch of Federales hanging around there and they bug people, shake 'em down, stuff like that. So I send Gus ahead to see if it's open. He comes back, gives me the thumbs-up, so we steam through Pie de la Cuesta and get up to where the first outpost of the Acapulco Police Department is. There's a guy in front of the station swinging his billy club in his white tropical uniform. He's looking up and down the road and all of a sudden he sees us and does this *fan-tas-tic*, movie-style double take, right? He looks at the top of the van and you can see his face go through the changes of "WOW!" and "Look what those people are doing!" and "No! It can't be!" just bam-bam-bam, and he finally just looks the other way because he can't process it. I mean the tarp is flapping, the gunny sacks are right there. What is an American doing hauling a van loaded with full gunny sacks? Carrying beans? Corn? Sunflower seeds? It could only be *one* thing.

And then we drove through the middle of Acapulco in 9 o'clock traffic on a Saturday morning. With Gus at this point trying to keep the road clear by *swerving* back and forth on the street about a block behind us, just blocking up traffic, right? People behind him are honking, cops are screaming at him, and he just says "No, no, man," he's going to cover us, right? All I want to do is go on through as inconspicuously as possible and he's creating a traffic jam so no one can get within half a block of me. Like that's going to do some good! I don't know what was going on in his head.

Finally we get to the house we'd rented. But ... the bus won't quite make it under the arch over the gate. By this time it's 10 o'clock in the morning and everybody in the neighborhood is up and around with nothing else in the world to do but hang around and stare at anything that happens. And here come the gringos: a car and another car towing a VW bus. None of these vehicles have they ever seen before at the house. When we were there, we'd been playing the Acapulco traveler trip, right? Me, my brother and Gus and tropical clothes, going to the beach in the afternoon, make 'em believe we're just tourists on vacation. And all of a sudden here we are: muddy, sweat running down our faces, exhausted, trying to get this load in under the arch. I'm on top of the van jumping up and down on these bags. "Scrunch 'em down another 2 inches and we got it made!" Stomp, stomp, stomp! Expecting a bag to split open and start spilling weed at any minute.

Finally we manage to start to ease this thing through the arch, and just about get it through but we're just a little shy on compaction, so the tarps start scraping off. And here are these bags, big, long gunny sacks with stems sticking out of them, fully exposed to view. We're situated down in this valley with hotels and apartment houses rising up on all sides, people are out on their decks having morning coffee — right in the bowl, the Hollywood Bowl! But finally we get the thing through the arch, lock the gate, go in the house and just *co*-llapse.

Chapter 14
Logistics And Hangups

The Acapulco house came with a maid and a gardener. The gardener came every day to weed and water, so there's no way to get this stuff out of the house without creating suspicion. Plus we had to keep the maid out of the room that had always been her quarters. One of my bedroom walls was just one stack of weed clear to the ceiling. I could sit on top of this stack of weed, the bags were stacked lengthwise up to the ceiling. And we had 'em every other available place in the house, too, all around the dining room, the front room, under the couches, in other bedrooms, *everywhere*. That's a lot of bulk and it was visible if you went in the house. You could smell it from the front yard!

The night we picked this stuff up, we were supposed be there at 9 o'clock, but we didn't even get the van we used until then and it's a three-hour drive from there to the pick-up spot. Meanwhile, it rains, they keep it as dry as they can under plastic but it gets wet anyway, so when we get back, in order not to ruin it we have to dry it out. If it gets packed in air-tight with moisture still in it, and there's any kind of bacteriological growth, it releases heat that's trapped inside and causes a mold that destroys it incredibly fast. So we had to dump this stuff all over the floor. We took up all the rugs and just dumped it out and fluffed it all up and kept turning it to let it dry. It had beautiful flowers, and we didn't want them to rot. So we had it spread out a foot deep all over the house. If anybody comes in any door, they have to step into a sea of pot. So we had to keep everybody out of the yard, keep the gate locked, keep the dog in the yard. Every time anybody came, one of us was "sick" or we were "having a party" or "recuperating from hangovers" — any excuse to keep people out.

139

We even told the truth a couple of times: "We're having a family fight. My brother Samuel is in the courtyard stabbing Goofy Gus." Really. I don't know what started it, shall we say they're both a little bit jumpy and defensive. See, Gus's quite a bit like my brother, but a couple of inches taller and a hundred pounds heavier. He's like the Orks in those Tolkien books. He's a mean dwarf but he's HUGE. He got into the trip because some friends of his had money invested in the trip. They weren't interested in going to Mexico but they wanted someone to watch their investment, so they sent him down, probably figuring that he looked like weight, like somebody who was really going to stand behind the action because he was so bulky. But he's really just a lard. I don't know what keyed it off, I think my brother said something to Gus and Gus said "I ain't taking any of your shit," and jumped up and started to go for his blade and they stood there back-and-forthing: "Cut me, man! Come on and cut me, motherfucker!" Just an insane, freakout trip.

So finally this great big spade cat George who was there to help with transportation gets in the middle and says "Hey, hey, no, no, no! Be cool, be cool," and gets them calmed down because they know if they don't cool it, George is going to take both fists and use 'em like big pile drivers and drive everybody's skulls against the wall, split 'em like eggs. George was a carpenter and woodworker. All he really wants to do in life is make beautiful stuff. He made a moon wall hanging for Tanya and a sun for the other chick down there that are just mind-blowers. He digs making wood sculpture for no other reason than to look beautiful. Or if you can find some use for it, that's groovy, too. We used one abstract piece he did for an incense holder. And the kind of trip he's into with smuggling, he can make some good money and then still have some materials left over for the stuff he really loves to do. He's perfectly cool, he wants the business to come down, he wants everybody to cool off, wants a good time and beautiful things and to sail through life, so George is no problem to me at all, he's a big help. He got into it after the guy with the boat backed out. He didn't want to risk his boat, but he sent George down to help. George is going to make us these big, heavy pieces of furniture with hollow places in them so you could hide the grass in them and they would be so big nobody would actually look inside them unless they broke. He showed up one day on the street in downtown Zihuatanejo — downtown! Whoa! You gotta see it, it's like out of a Western movie, dirt streets, very little wood aside from the sidewalks, the buildings are all that cruddy brick made in kilns fired with corn husks, so they don't get very hot and the bricks are just basically mud. They build houses with it because it's cheap but the bricks will not hold up, so they have to coat 'em with cement and then paint 'em some beautiful color like robin's egg blue or greenish aqua or pink.

So George comes up to me on the street one day and introduces himself and says he's looking for Mika Airth. Well, I was expecting George but I wasn't expecting a 50-year-old spade who looked like a cop, so I said, "Okay, let's go have a beer." I'm wondering if the cat with the boat got busted and set me up because George really looked like a cop. He's 50 years old and he doesn't come on like the cats I'm used to doing business with. I'm used to doing business with guys my own age. We go have a beer and he sounds all right but at first I'm not sure his system is any good. But as we talk it sounds better and better and I figure he's probably okay and maybe it's worth taking the chance. I'm pretty anxious to get moving and get the hell out of there. So I take him to the house and get him stoned, he smokes grass, he really digs it, he's okay. So that's how George got into it. Over the next couple of days we talk a lot and I find out that a really good friend in San Francisco has worked with him using the same setup and was successful with it, which is what really sold me on the idea. I found out that George knew a lot of the same people I did and they'd been successful with his furniture approach.

George had been in the Merchant Marine, which is where he learned smuggling. He tells me that the Merchant Marine — talk about *smugglers*! He's been just about everywhere. We were talking about going to the city of Buenaventura sometime, in Colombia. It's like a Latin American version of what Shanghai used to be: jewels, drugs and every kind of contraband happening. See, there are a lot of gold, diamond and emerald mines in these countries and the cats who work there steal, just like the African diamond mines trip. The stuff they steal usually ends up going through Buenaventura, there's a big black market scene. After hearing George talk about it, I thought I'd like to go dig it sometime, but where I'm at right now, I'd rather not. The way I feel right now, I don't think I'll be involved with any smuggling for a long time, if ever.

As for Goofy Gus, he really is goofy. He's in a stage of metamorphosis from a Chicago gangster sort of cat into a pacifistic, hippie sort of a cat, but he's still a lot more Chicago than San Francisco, if you know what I mean. Like he talks with relish about violence he's been involved in, he still gets a thrill talking about that. I know he has moral equivocations about what he's done, but that tough guy thing is still there, he grew up in a rough Chicago neighborhood and he's still carrying that load. I got him and I didn't even know who he was actually in with. The guy who sent him, I didn't even know he knew these kind of people. I knew he was from Chicago, but he was groovy and I never figured he'd send a guy like Gus in my direction. Gus turned out to be a real drag. He's freaky. He's stuck in Mexico longer than he expected and he's just freaked out. He's weird. He's nasty mostly to get off his frustrations over being isolated and trapped in Mexico

142

because he really doesn't want to be there. That just stirs up a lot of trouble because he'll make a nasty crack for a reason completely unrelated to the nasty crack but someone will take the remark as something personal and they'll get into a hassle about it. Like he'll insult somebody's chick — and in a gross way. I mean, he's pretty gross. I don't know exactly how he did it, because he never did it when I was around, but I'd come back from doing something somewhere else and hear about these things.

The way he got into it in the first place was it turned out there was some Chicago money involved in his scene. See, I had some bread and halfway through the trip I ran out. That happened half a dozen times and each time I had to get more bread somewhere. So one time I called this guy who'd put some money in the year before. He'd put money in then well into the trip, and it took me a long time to get him his share back but I did, so he knew that sooner or later I could get it done. So I called him again and he said yeah and sent somebody down with $2,500. About a month after I got the bread, which is getting to be a long time, this guy starts feeling anxious, starts worrying that maybe I'm not going to make it this time.

What I finally find out is, it's not just this one cat getting uptight, he got his investment cash from somebody who's the son of a bookie who's involved with The Outfit in Chicago. Not only that, but the son is about to go to jail behind not having enough to pay somebody off. So his old man the bookie is saying "Listen, let me lean on this guy a little." So that's where the real pressure was from. And the last thing in the world I would *ever* knowingly do is get involved with those people. For a myriad of reasons. First, I know how they operate. If you don't make your deadline they either make it so physically plain that you have to get the bread somewhere, that you rob a store if you have to. Or they charge so much interest that it's just not worth it. Besides which, I don't dig 'em. They're a bunch of fucking pigs. They come out of the same bag as the pigs. They operate the same way, doing business with them is just like doing business with the cops. It was just pure accident that I got involved with them because I didn't know my friend was getting his bread from them. They were bad news. They were talking about sending somebody to break my hands, shit like that. That's what the guy said to me on the phone: "First they'll break your hands, then they'll break your kneecaps, then they'll give you another week, then they'll break all your toes." So let 'em find me. Gus isn't going to do it because he's outnumbered and out of touch with them. Besides, they wouldn't be fronting me their money if they could do the trip themselves. They can't do it, they don't know how, they're a bunch of dumb old farts. No, really! The only way they can get the bread is at the point of a gun, they're not smart enough to put together a rational trip. All that smack they're involved in, it's always some other cat that knows how to do it that they get into somehow. Then they just make the pressure so heavy on him that he winds up saying "Fuck it! You can have the business, you can have the setup, just leave me alone." Either that or they just — he just disappears.

Two or three years ago there was a big heroin bust in New York where the smugglers were using a custom Citroen. The guy who originally had that scene was a smart cat and a good smuggler. For instance, he knew that the customs people have a mockup of every ordinary car. They know where the hidden space in a Mustang is, they know where the hidden space in a Volkswagen is, they know any standard car. So he figures he'll just buy a vehicle overseas and have it shipped back, but some kind of vehicle they aren't familiar with. His small package is worth enough to make buying an expensive vehicle a reasonable expense, so he buys a $10,000 custom-made Citroen to smuggle in his heroin. He puts it on a ship somewhere in France and it comes into New York and they unload the car and he picks it up and sells the smack to The Syndicate. And then, I don't know if they get to him by pressuring him or offering a lot of money or what, but he tells them what the trip is and they force him out or scare him away or something. Then they send the *same car* back and ship it across again and pick it up and unload it and send it back again on the same fucking boat! They do that seven times because they haven't got enough brains to figure out that "Hey, that load is worth $3 million, maybe we'd better spend another 10 grand on a different car." And of course finally the Customs people see this same car coming in every time the boat docks and — being pretty god-damned stupid themselves because it takes them seven times! — finally the light clicks on and they decide they better check this car out.

Not only have they used the hidden compartment that the original guy had built in — which, Christ, believe me, the Customs people never would have found — but they stuck more into the spare tire and other really obvious places because they figured "Well, it works so good we don't even have to worry about it, all we gotta do is conceal it a little bit and they won't even look." So that's how smart The Syndicate cats are. And that's how smart Customs is. Listen, a Customs officer said in an article I read in San Francisco Magazine, I think, or maybe in one of the airline magazines, that 99 percent of the people they catch is on tip-offs — the other 1 percent is pure accident. In other words, they're looking for something they hardly ever find. They can't check every package and crate coming into this country and until they can, they're not going to stop the flow of weed or anything else. There are too many people into it. They busted a state senator from Maryland coming in with 17 pounds of hash. There are senators and bankers carrying around fucking kilos in their briefcases! But the dodo Outfit, how smart are they? It's incredible. I don't care if you use this either, because as far as I'm concerned, anything that helps keep anybody from getting involved with The Outfit or with anybody who thinks like The Outfit is groovy with me.

Anyway, that's how Goofy Gus got into our trip, he was the big, ugly surprise attached to the Outfit's investment. It was yet another hassle dealing with him while trying to finish this trip.

Chapter 15
Moving The Product

We had to move the weed from Acapulco to Mexico City. We knew if we put it in suitcases we'd have 50 suitcases. If it's that many, I don't care where you're sending it, it shouts out "50 SUITCASES OF WEED!" So since George knows how to build shipping crates we decided to make big, unmanageable boxes and label them "Spanish Colonial Furniture." It'll be heavy, everybody will believe it and we won't have any Customs problems getting the weed to Mexico City. Then George can make the furniture in Mexico City and we can put the weed in the furniture and ship it from there. You wouldn't dare just ship a crate full of weed, they open all the crates leaving Mexico just to check what's inside. We figured they wouldn't rip into George's massive crates.

We built two HUGE crates, beauties, man! They were made of wet pine, 3 feet wide and 4 feet high and almost 10 feet long. They must have weighed 400 or 500 pounds each. We put 350 kilos of weed in each one, so they weighed almost a thousand pounds each. If anybody asked we would just say "Oh, Spanish Colonial wardrobes, 3-inch maple." Then we hire a truck. It takes 10 guys to get the crates into the truck and shift it around so it's in place. But we manage to get them loaded up and head for Mexico City.

And that was where I almost blew the whole trip because I couldn't get the money that I'd had wired to me.

I'd sent Tanya and Domingo ahead to line up a house on a Thursday, and on Friday we got into Mexico City. I leave the truck and the eight people who were with me at that point at the house they'd lined up and I go to the telegraph office to pick up the money I'd had wired down to take care of expenses. When I get to the telegraph office, I discover that although in almost any small town in

Mexico you don't even have to have any I.D. to pick up money at a telegraph office, if you're in Mexico City you have to have your visa or your passport, *period*. So the money was there, but I'd had it wired to a phony name because I'd been using a phony I.D. that fit my description. I didn't have any other I.D. for this scene, because I'd had the money sent to this other name on the phony I.D. I don't really like to use my own name. I got this I.D. by way of a corner on Fillmore Street in San Francisco where you can buy papers from wallets that thieves have lifted. They take the money, then sell the papers. For 10 bucks you can buy a set. You tell them what description you need and give 'em a phone number and when a guy gets what you need, you got your papers. So those are the papers I had. The guy's description matched mine and there was a place for a picture where I put my photo in, but these papers won't work in Mexico City. Even in Acapulco you can go in with your AAA card and claim money, but it turns out that in Mexico City with all its swingin' sophistication you have to have a passport or visa. That's all they'll accept. Not a birth certificate, not a membership card for the New York Stock Exchange, which I had. So the money's there, but I can't get it.

To get it I would have had to call the guy who arranged it, then he would have to get the guy who actually sent the money to take his receipt to the telegraph office and tell them the person he sent it to isn't able to pick it up, so he has to change the recipient. Then they would have sent a wire to Mexico City and I could use my own papers, my passport, or someone else who had one, like George, could use his to pick it up. So once the recipient change got to Mexico City you'd think they'd release the money, but they won't because the employees screw around so much with the money orders that, for instance, if I was in Acapulco and I got a wire for $2,000, the Acapulco office would send a wire back to the U.S. office to confirm that

that amount of money was from there, and if that was confirmed, then they'd release it.

That means I can't get that money for at least a couple of days of this stuff, and then only if I keep on it 24 hours a day, even though I'm in the nation's capital. Meanwhile, I have this trucker waiting at the house I'm supposed to be renting and he's already charging double because he's already waited six hours while I've been trying to get the money. So I owe the trucker a thousand pesos right off, plus there's nothing to pay for the house. Meanwhile I've got these crates of weed sitting there and eight people depending on me to get them located somewhere and preserve the business trip we're all enmeshed in. Now it looks like the whole thing is about to blow up in our faces. That's when I almost blew it, because after I found out I couldn't get the money I just sort of drove around Mexico City for a couple of hours in a daze, unable to think of one fucking thing I could do. I was as low at that point as I've ever been in my life. I finally just parked and sat there and was ready to give it all up as a lost cause. I've never come so close to completely blowing it. But I sat there for a while and started to get myself together and thought "I gotta do something, all these people are waiting."

Then I thought of a friend I met on a trip down there once who has a publishing business in Mexico City. So I call him but he's in Guadalajara and won't be back for a month. The cat I talk to on the phone doesn't know how to reach him, but I also know his son. It turns out his son has had a split-up with his father and the guy I'm talking to doesn't know where he's living but he has been over to the son's girlfriend's house and there's a good chance, this being a Friday afternoon, that the son will be there.

So I get the address and go over and sure enough, the guy is there. All I need is a couple of thousand pesos and this kid is rich so I figure I can borrow the bread, but it turns out that with this split-up with his father and the fact that he hasn't been working too much because he's a struggling actor, he doesn't have any money. His girlfriend doesn't have any either, she's waiting for him to get back together with his father to get his father's money back into their scene so she can feel comfortable enough to marry him. So neither one has any money, but he says "I think I know someone who'll buy your car." So I said "Okay, I'll sell it cheap I need this money right away."

In the meantime, the truckers are freaking out, they're afraid I'm not going to come back with the bread, they want to seize the merchandise, the "furniture" that we have, to hold in lieu of the money and they want to open the crates to see exactly what they've got for collateral. So I shoot over to the used car lot that this friend's son recommends. And first of all, this car's not my car, the car and all the papers are in the name of a 43-year-old American Negro, which it says very plainly, his picture is on the papers. So I get to the car lot and say "I want to sell this car, I'll sell it *very* cheap." And the cat looks over the car and says "Do you have the papers?" I hand him the papers, he looks at them and hands them back and says "I don't think I can buy this car." I ask why. He says, "It will get me in a lot of trouble trying to get the papers straightened out and everything. To sell it, I'd have to take it apart and sell it in pieces and I'm not really interested in doing that." So I'm wondering what the hell I can do and he must have been able to tell I was in bad trouble because he says "But I'll loan you 2,000 pesos on your word." *Blew* my mind, man! Here I am, a *gringo* who's trying to sell him a car illegally. He knows this, he knows I'm in some kind of jam. At this point I'm one scruffy-looking cat, the car is real scruffy looking, there's a door missing on one side, it's crumpled up and in the trunk, the car is only a couple of years old but it's beat, really beat. And he's going to *lend* me a couple of thousand pesos on my word! He's the only person that's loaned me money in a long time that got it back really *fast*. I paid him back as soon as I could because he blew my mind so bad. This was a Mexican used car dealer, loans me 2,000 pesos the first time he's ever laid eyes on me! That publisher's son's recommendation must have come pretty high.

So I take the money, go over, pay the truck driver. But the woman whose home we're going to rent has decided that before we can move in — after seeing what she's seen, with the truck driver freaking out and all the people sitting there waiting for me saying "Oh, he'll be back in just a minute, he'll be back any time, don't worry, it's a sure thing!" and Domingo almost gets into a fist fight with the caretaker for this house, so when I do get back the landlady has decided "Unless I have a couple of months' rent, a co-signer and a deposit, I'm not going to let these people move in, they're just too weird," which runs it up to the point where we can't handle it. So we give the truck driver some more money and say "Wait here, we'll be right back." And we go around the corner and about three blocks to another house that I had my old lady and Domingo check out. We figured something might go wrong with the first place, so we had this other one in sight. We fast-talk the maid at this second house into letting us drop the crates off there on the pretext that we're on our way to see the woman who's leasing it to sign the lease. We start unloading the stuff and the maid's husband, who's the caretaker for this house, shows up and says "You can't do this! No! Stop!" And we're pushing these huge crates off the truck and we're just "No, man, we're unloading here. Help or get out of the way, if one of these boxes falls on you, you're a dead man!"

So he gets out of the way and runs to the phone, he's going to call the owners and find out what's going on. I send Tanya with him and tell her to get on the phone and just stall, say anything, stall long enough for us to get this stuff off the truck and get the truck away, then even if the landlord comes over we can say "I'm sorry, as soon as we can hire another truck we'll get this stuff out of here." We figure the owner won't mess with it no matter what he thinks it is. Even if he figures out we're smugglers and we've just dropped these huge crates of weed in his front yard, nonetheless it's *his* front yard and he's not going to want to try to explain to the Federales that it's not his 600 keys of weed. So Tanya stalls the landlady and we get the stuff unloaded and the truck splits and we sit back and wait, figuring the landlord's going to show up any minute. The landlady isn't going to come now because she was going to handle the rental, but it got too complicated, so the old man's going to come.

Sure enough, he drives up. In a Mercedes. He's in an alpaca golf sweater, button-down collar, wing-tips, a real Spanish-looking guy. I look at him and think "Oh, yeah, straight arrow's here." And he is calm, he is really calm. I later find out he speaks six languages, was born in Seville, Spain, was on the Porsche economics squad at Stuttgart, he's been around, ain't nothin' going to shake him up. He's all cool precision. He says "What's going on here?" I tell him my story about having to have a place because the truck driver was going to charge me double and I'm in a bind and so on and so forth and he says, "All right. You may leave your crates here. I'm not going to rent the house to you. You'll have to have them out by Monday morning." So then I know it doesn't make any difference what he thinks is in those crates, he isn't going to try to explain to anyone how 680 kilos of weed got there, he's just going to make sure I get my boxes out of there as fast and clean as possible. So we go check into a hotel fairly sure that when we get back the stuff's going to be there and he won't call the heat, which is exactly how it turned out.

So that was Friday and we left it there till Tuesday. We thought we had a place lined up to rent as a workshop to set up George to make the furniture but Tanya has gone on this trip with Domingo, right? She's running around holding hands with him and stuff like that. And the people who are renting places are real straight, Mexico City, Castilian Spaniards. They see this American chick and this Indian and they say "We want six months rent in advance and two co-signers and ..." you know, just "no." Altogether we moved the weed to Acapulco, then to Mexico City to this guy's house, then to a storage warehouse, then to another town. That's a lot of moving when the crates are that big and heavy.

We had a whole lot of hassles looking for places to stash the stuff and get the furniture and crates made. Because at this point you have my brother whose hair is brown and real long; you have this chick he picked up in Acapulco who'd been staying with the people we rented the VW bus from and who's a plastic hippie kind of chick who spends three hours getting herself made up in the morning. Like I take one pair of pants to the cleaners when we get back to Phoenix and she's got sixteen items to go and we've only been in town three days. She changes clothes six or seven times a day! Then you got Tanya and Sally, the third-pillow chick, who are both blondes, and Domingo the Indian, and George, a 50-year-old, 250-pound, booming-voiced spade. And you got Goofy Gus, a huge troll with page-boy-length hair. It's a set of people that Mexico City establishment cats just aren't used to. So we have trouble locating houses.

On Friday night Sally and I checked into the hotel where George, Domingo and Tanya were. We got the room across the hall from them. Then you got Gus, my brother and his chick Marilyn, Miss Plastic Hippie. They got the room next to ours. We checked in separately but the hotel people obviously figured out we must be together. It was insane! Gus would wake up in the middle of the night paranoid about something or other and knock on doors and

153

wake everybody up and we'd have to have a conference to straighten things out. People were running off here and there to check on houses and get away from each other for a while. When we'd come through the lobby the staff would just look at us blank-eyed. We were trouble to them, but we were paying trouble, so they endured us. With the language thing — Domingo was the only one of us who spoke very much Spanish and he was an Indian who couldn't read — and all the hassles trying to get places lined up to rent dealing with a bunch of Castilian Spaniards, plus all the personal hassles going on with me and Tanya and Domingo and Sally, it was hard, baby, *hard.* *Muy malo.*

We've got 680 keys of weed sitting in a warehouse inside plastic bags inside the crates. It contains a certain amount of moisture and it's hot in Mexico City, so I could just picture the stuff starting to sweat in that plastic. If it sweats in there, pretty soon it starts to mold and once it starts that, you have to be God Himself to save it. I once got some kilos that were packed into cars in Tijuana on a Wednesday afternoon and came across the border on Thursday night, got into L.A. on Friday morning, and I had them by about mid-day Saturday and put them into a stash. I went over to look at them Sunday night. When they came into town they weren't hot and sweaty but by Sunday night when I opened one of the suitcases and put my hand on one of those bricks, it was so hot, your impulse was to pull back your hand. The hotter it gets, the faster the mold grows. It could actually conceivably spontaneously combust if it doesn't sweat itself out. So now I have all this weed sitting in crates in a warehouse and can't find a house to rent.

First of all, any place where we can stay and not bring down all kinds of heat is real expensive. Plus it's hard to look for places in Mexico City with just one car. By now we've had to sell the other car because we were having problems with having enough bread to keep this whole

154

tribe going. Selling the car was how we paid for the truck to get the crates out of that guy's yard and into storage and that was why it took until Tuesday instead of Monday to get it done. It was the car I'd tried to sell before, a '67 or '68 Chevrolet with one door on and one door off and an American registration with Illinois plates. I suspect it was stolen to begin with. The cat who had the papers was traveling under a phony name and it's illegal to sell the car in Mexico but we have to sell it somehow to survive.

So we go out along this street in Mexico City where all the junkers and auto parts houses are, hoping we'll run into somebody who'll break the car down for parts and then we can kill two birds with one stone because we'll get some money and we won't have to worry about trying to take the car back into the States with phony papers. But it's not that easy to illegally sell a car in Mexico City unless you know somebody. So we start looking for someone. George and I go to that part of town and start hitting on people. George isn't doing too much, just pushing me out front, and I don't know what's going on, all I know is I've got a car to sell. I approach people first by telling them I've got this car and I don't really want to take it back to the States, I'd like to either fix it or sell it. That way nobody can say "You're breaking the law." We hit on five cats and they all like the car, it's cheap compared with what it would cost to buy it legally, but they'll have to break it down and part it out and they aren't really interested in that much effort, they've already got their trips taken care of, it would just be too much work and too dangerous if they get caught.

Finally we run into a guy who takes us to another guy's house who takes us to another guy who's the dispatcher for the garbage pickup people, and he takes us into an area of town by the athletic stadium and tells us there's a guy who lives on the left-hand side of that street over there in a house set back from the street who will know somebody who'll buy this car for our price. Turns out he's not there, we have to come back at 11 o'clock at night. And I mean this is a rough part of Mexico City, we don't know what we're getting into — well, you never do but we figure whatever it is, we can handle it. So we go over there at 11 at night and knock on the door and a guy says it's the next house down, and this happens again, and just when we think we've found the right house three street patrol cops on bicycles ride up and want to be helpful. I mean, they really want to be helpful, thinking we're tourists, clean-looking, looking for somebody's house. The guy we're looking for, his front is as a furniture maker, so we tell the cops we're looking for Antonio the furniture maker, we're buyers from a store in the United States and we want to get some of his furniture, but we have a limited amount of time — because look, it's weird, it's 11 at night, buyers looking for somebody? — but the cops aren't familiar with how business is done by people from the States so they help us by knocking on doors, waking people up until pretty soon everybody in the neighborhood is awake.

After a while, this little Mexican guy comes out from behind this shed, a little guy with a baseball cap with the bill turned up, wearing moontan-grey pants, his shirt hanging open, wiping the sleep out of his eyes. As soon as I see him I know he's the cat, just by his vibrations and the way he carries himself. He's looking at the cops and looking this whole scene over and it's like he's the cat who's really onto it, he's dealing, man, and he's dressed poor because he wants to look poor, but that's not really where he's at, he's into something, he's the guy who'll buy this car. He walks out and there's a little game with the heat because he's doing something illegal and we're there to ask him to do it but the heat are standing right there. They ask him if he's Antonio the furniture maker and he says yeah. And I had given them the name of somebody who'd given me his name so I told him that, and he said he didn't know that person. I mentioned a street a block away as the street

156

we were given and he says yeah, that's a block over, you've got the wrong furniture maker. And every time there's a lapse in the conversation and the police are looking away, this guy is pinning me and smiling, so I know he's the guy. So the cops think we're lost and we thank them and go back to our hotel but go back to see Antonio the next morning. We drive up and no sooner shut the engine off than he walks out. *"Buenos dias, que pasa?"* and all that.

He says to do business we have to go to this other place in an even rattier part of town, but it all feels okay so we go there and talk about papers and how we can make them look like something legitimate and then he has to go get the bread for the car. Meanwhile, we have a deadline, we have to be back at the house by 2 p.m. to get the weed out of this guy's yard or we're going to have a big hassle. The trucker's still over there waiting and if he doesn't get his money soon he'll start raising hell and attract unwanted attention. At noon they get back from the bank with the money and it takes half an hour to get a cab and another half hour to get back to the hotel, so we have an hour to hire another truck and get it to the place and pay the original driver and get him gone and then get the other truck in and load the crates and get them out. And we make it, man, by the skin of our fucking teeth!

And by the way, that car sale led to the only good times I had in Mexico City, with the family of the guy who bought the car. They were outasight people! There must be, I don't know, 10 kids in the family, and they're playing Ranchero music the first time we go over there. They talk with us for a while trying to figure out who we are, where we're at, and then they put on their only Beatles album for us and cook us breakfast, including steak and eggs, and just treat us royally. They invite us to come and stay there if we want to get out of the hotel, they won't charge anything, they'd just like to have our company. We really got it on with them, they were some of the grooviest people I met the whole time I was in Mexico. Because they just laid it out on the line: "You're a criminal, I'm a criminal, I dig you, we're having a good time together, if you want to stay here, you're welcome and you know nothing will happen to you as long as you're here." I'd be delighted to see them again, they were really groovy. Like one time their little girl comes in and brings us flowers, just really nice things like that.

And that's where I met the Michoacana. When she finally got busted it was front-page news in Mexico City. She's from Michoacan, maybe 40 years old, she's been dealing weed and cocaine in Mexico City for 25 years or so, she started when she was 12 or 13. She's a tough broad, man, I mean just one tough broad. I was with her one time when some drunk came up and started hitting on her and trying to man-handle her. I was on the other side of the room and I started over to help her out but before I could even get there she came up off her chair and hit this guy in the face with her fist and knocked him stiff. She wasn't just slapping at him or pushing, she pulled her arm down alongside her and "CRACK!" let him have it in the mouth. Then pulled out her knife in case he got up. "Out of here, you! Crawl out that door!" And he did. I would have too, if I were him. Because she would have killed him "POP!" just like that.

I met her through this family we'd met. She was running with people who were friendly, who were her friends and when she was with friends, she was outasight. We'd sit around and get stoned and drink and have a good time. But if she got on somebody's case — I mean, I've known some tough women, I've knocked around with people who if they are women, they have to be able to maintain, but the Michoacana was incredible. If her man was in prison, I believe she'd bend bars to get him out, that kind of woman.

158

Chapter 16
Finding A Place

So we had some good times with those people, but otherwise, Mexico City was just a big blister. Because everybody in our tribe by now is uptight with just about everyone else, right? Just really uptight. Finally we decide that the only way we're going to get into the kind of place we need is by having Domingo find one. Then he can rent it and we can move in and do our thing, probably without getting hassled. But he's on some kind of ego trip and won't just go into one of the neighborhoods in Mexico City where we thought he could find something fast enough and cheap enough. He figures he's already done his part so he's just going to sit back and start pulling strings. He's getting really arrogant. Finally I had to come down on him like 10 tons of shit.

One afternoon at the hotel he started in on one of his trips about not helping move, he wasn't going to get involved, but he still wanted his piece of the profit. I just said, "Hey, listen, motherfucker!" in the clearest gutter Spanish I could summon, "You get off my ass, brother, or I'm going to tear your head right off the top of your neck!" He was sitting in a chair and his hand started to move for his back pocket for his knife and I thought "Okay, you just get it out because I'm ready for you and when I see that blade clear your back pocket I'm going to hit you with this chair I'm standing behind so hard that that I'll bury the fucking leg in your fucking brain." I was *pissed*. I already hate him because he's getting it on with Tanya. Not only that, but he's responsible for the financial situation being so screwed up. And he thinks he's going to ride *my* ass? I'm past the point of being ridden anywhere by anyone. I'm wired up tight, I don't care what happens because I want to get that anger out, it's driving me crazy! And he's right on the edge of giving me the opportunity to just whale on his fucking ass. My brother is on the other side of the hotel room and sees what's happening and in about half a second he's holding Domingo by his shirtfront with his knife blade on Domingo's throat saying "Move, motherfucker, and I'm going to cut your windpipe wide open!" But George comes in again and smooths it over as best it can be smoothed and we finally settle down and go on about our business.

Meanwhile, that weed is sitting in the warehouse in danger of molding, so we decide to just get out of town, go where things aren't so sophisticated and uptight. We rent a place in Querétaro, about a hundred miles northwest of Mexico City. We get the downstairs of the home of a Mexican and his wife and two teen-age daughters. That's not too cool for our purposes but there's a little sort of apartment out back and a workshop, and we told them we were going to be making furniture. The owner was easy-going and rented us the place. Then we moved everything up there, all George's equipment, so he can make tables with built-in spaces for the weed and decorate them and crate them and we'll ship 'em to the United States.

I and Samuel will go back to the U.S. to receive it and make sure it gets through all the brokerage houses and shipping processes. Everyone else will stay in Mexico and take care of that end of shipping. At this point, Domingo and Tanya are living in the little apartment in back, which is bugging me more than a little. In the main house are my brother, who wants to kill Domingo so bad, if only I'd let him, and his lady Marilyn. All I would have had to say was "Hey, do you mind?" and he would have with great gusto and pleasure slit Domingo's throat. I mean I had to haul Samuel off of Domingo many times just to keep the whole trip together. So I have that situation plus Sally, who still wants me to be her man but I'm not interested anymore because breaking up with Tanya has me so torn up. And then Gus and George, who I thought were both fairly level right then, but that turned out to be a miscalculation.

160

So George is supposed to stay there to make the furniture and crates and Tanya and Domingo are supposed to make sure everything gets done right and watch their part of the load because Domingo is worried about what kind of retaliation might be coming from me for his involvement with Tanya. He's expecting something, so he doesn't just want to leave all of this in our hands, he's afraid he won't get his cut. Plus ostensibly for me, the reason for having them there is to see that Gus and George don't try any rip-offs. Sally's going to stay to help keep track of things for me and help me, if necessary and if she can, until things get far enough along that I can get her home. Samuel and his lady Marilyn and I are going to split in Gus's Kharman Ghia with all our stuff and go back north to receive the shipment.

So we split. Unknown to me my brother and his chick have decided it would be really a drag to not bring any of this really tasty weed with us. I'm on a big trip to make sure that we're clean, because we have a lot invested and we can't afford getting busted at the border with a lid or something like that. When we pull up to the border station about midnight it's closed. It's not going to open until 8 in the morning, so the three of us have to sleep in the Ghia. It's about 20 degrees outside and we have no winter clothes, we just have tropical stuff because when we went down, we figured we'd spend all our time in a tropical zone and then fly back. So there we sit in the Ghia, freezing our asses off until the border station opens. Which gives me plenty of time to berate myself. The border finally opens and we pull up there all sleepy-eyed and they search the car and the luggage. Then on the other side I want to stop and get some kind of nonprescription tranquilizer because I am a wreck, I mean a total fucking physical wreck. I'm 6-1 and I weighed 170 pounds when I went down, and when we got back I weighed 120. I lost 50 fucking pounds! So when I come out of the store I say, "Jesus Christ, I wish we had some weed," and Samuel and Marilyn say "Oh, we have!" I say "What do you mean?" My brother says "Well, we couldn't just throw it away, we figured they wouldn't find it." He'd taken out a headlight and taped a lid on the back and put it back in. And they often check headlights! I mean they check in fender wells and so on because they know that one. They've ripped the panels out of enough cars and found enough weed to know people do that. I just said "*Fuck*, man!" And all Samuel said was, "I just knew they weren't going to look."

We should have been thoroughly searched. I had a mustache and I had decided a few weeks before that I wasn't getting any more haircuts and I was starting to look scruffy. I had about a three-day beard growth. My brother had long hair and Marilyn looked like a hippie chick and we were in this old car after being there for months — but they hardly checked us. Oh, they carefully went through the suitcases and looked under the dash and squeezed the seats and hit the door panels and felt the weight of the doors and looked in the glove compartment and under the mats, but they never searched any of us personally and they didn't start taking the car apart, which fortunately for us they don't unless they have good reason. Besides that, most smugglers take more care about how they look and what kind of vehicle they're driving. They would never use a vehicle like ours because it seemed doubtful at every moment whether it would make it or break down. There were holes in the back floorboards big enough to drop coffee cans through. But it ran like a dream the whole trip, only sputtered once.

So we get to Phoenix and wait for the first shipment, which had been sent before we left Acapulco to move to Mexico City and went through all our hassles there. While all that was going on, this unit was supposed to be in transit. So we figured by the time we got to Phoenix, it would be there within a couple of days, the

162

broker might even have it when we get there. So I start calling the broker. I give him some story about my aunt being in Mexico, she's sending some furniture for our new home and my wife wants it because she's going to have a dinner party next week and we really need it. Actually, we're all anxious to get that first unit in order to get enough bread to everybody that things will lighten up a bit, at least people won't have to worry about having enough money to go out and have a few drinks or buy food and essentials. So I tell the broker this tale so he won't be suspicious if I keep checking back real often. I don't want it to sit around long after the broker gets it, I want to keep it moving because things can happen. A little bit of weed might happen to leak out a little crack where something has been dropped and broken, but if the shipment keeps moving fast enough, by the time somebody figures out where that little bit of spilled weed came from, it's already moved too fast for them to catch up with it. That's happened to friends of mine, and I've seen it happen the other way. One time it got to a certain point and everybody relaxed and figured "It's safe now," and let it sit on a freight dock for three or four days. By the time they went to pick it up, somebody in Mexico had noticed that little bit of weed where that crate had been sitting and figured out where it was going. When they went to pick it up, the heat was waiting.

But I start calling this broker and he doesn't have anything. This goes on for a couple of weeks, so I send a telegram to the people in Mexico saying "Call me at this number at this time." They call and I ask what happened, the broker hasn't received any notifications and hasn't gotten the crate. It turned out that it took over a month since the shipment was put on a truck in Acapulco until it got to the brokerage house at the border. Over a *month*! It had been in transit for three weeks when I started calling the brokerage, so I told my people in Mexico they'd better try to track it down and they said okay. They were supposed to call me when they found out. I waited another week, and they finally called and asked if it had arrived. I said no and asked if they'd checked on it and they said no, they were all afraid to go start inquiring about it because if it had been gone that long, the heat must be on it. I said "Hey! Use your head! All you have to do is call the freight line and ask them, then call back and let me know what you find out. And I'll have the broker at this end try to trace it, too. There's no possible way they can know. Just find out what's happening!"

About three days later Tanya calls back and says, "Well, it's finally shipped from Mexico City." She said they had lost the shipping instructions so it had been sitting on their dock in Mexico City while they waited for someone to contact them. Four days after it finally shipped it was at the border. If they'd done what I told them weeks before that it would have been there two weeks earlier. But it's finally in the brokerage house in Nogales and they have instructions to get it to an address near Phoenix, in a real small town outside of Phoenix I'd set up with my brother. He and another guy were going to sell part of the first shipment to raise some cash. They were at this other guy's house, an outasight place, a mind-blowing house like Donovan should be living in. Antique furniture, velvet drapes, real crystal chandeliers, hand-carved wooden chairs with lions and scenery carved into the backs.

But then came a new complication: I and Samuel got into it. It was over some stuff that happened when I was 12 years old and he was two years younger and I would beat the shit out of him. He'd always had it in for me because of that, he'd been carrying that grudge for a long, long time, plus he had been doing a lot of work on this Mexico trip and hadn't seen any bread for it yet — neither had anybody else, but that just added to his resentment. I was physically depleted and he figured he was ready and started trying to goad me into a fight every way he could.

He'd slap me, back me into corners, insult Tanya, our friends, our parents. He did everything possible, even running down our recently dead father. It was his father, too, and he didn't mean 90 percent of what he was saying, he was just trying to get me to react. Finally I punched him and we got into it. At one point this other cat who's supposed to be helping with the weed is standing in the doorway watching us fight. My brother has me down on the floor with a piece of pipe across my throat strangling me. I'm gasping to this cat "Hey, man! Pull him off! He's killing me!" And this cat just stands there. But finally I get him off me and I get a scissors-grip around his ribs and a hand on his throat and choke him until he's practically unconscious and squeeze his ribs until they separate — and he's still pounding on me! He was working his elbows up and down on my legs. I had charley horses so bad I could barely walk for about four days. I had a black eye, knots all over my head and face, I was aching. We just kept on until we were both too exhausted to fight any more. Then we went out and had a cup of coffee and talked it over.

But after the fight, things were pretty heavy around the place. It was a pretty volatile situation. There were a whole bunch of people counting on this thing getting done, so I'm asking myself if I should bring it in through my brother and this guy after Samuel tried to kill me and this guy just stood and watched. I figure I'd better not trust them. I don't know if I can really prevent them from getting it because I don't know if the broker's already sent it off to the house where Samuel's supposed to pick it up. I get to a phone and tell the broker that it's too late, my wife insisted I get her another set of furniture because of this dinner party, so we're going to give that shipment of furniture to her sister, who lives in Northern California. I give him a nonexistent address about 40 miles outside San Francisco and tell him to ship it there freight-collect. He says okay and tells me what freight line he's going to ship with.

So that's taken care of, but I'm in Phoenix with no money — I mean, NO money, like not one cent — and I have to get to San Francisco fast in order to protect everybody's interests. I lay some kind of story on my brother and this other guy and get 20 bucks from them and jump in the Ghia and race off for San Francisco.

Chapter 17
Getting It Done

I drove until I got to Santa Cruz and went through the Santa Cruz mountains to this guy's house who had put some money into the trip. I was wasted, really wasted from the stress and the drive. I thought I would tell him, "Okay, Greg, I'm finally back and the thing is set up, these shipments are going to be coming in, so if you want to handle picking them up and offing the weed, you can do that." But when I got to his house, I just really cracked up, I was crying, really freaked out. I stayed there a few hours but the people there just weren't interested in helping finish the trip. So I split to another friend's, Jeannie's, to keep checking with the broker on the first unit. When it finally did come, I moved up to the country and mostly from that point on I was just offing these pieces and paying people back for bread they'd put into it, and trying to get my health back.

By then there was 10 or 12 grand invested and I couldn't really sell it to best advantage because there was so much pressure to pay off people who were waiting for their money. It's hard to be realistic about how much we could have made if it had gone down the way it was originally supposed to. There's a certain amount of money in a trip that can be made if you can sell 600 or 700 kilos at the best price. You can make a *pile* of money if that happens. But everyone had been waiting so long and was so anxious to get their money that it got sold cheaper than it could have. We could have made about $100,000. A lot of it would have gone to other people. As it happened, what I initially got and sold mostly went to other people. Each investor got a certain amount out of what I made to show that they were eventually going to get their money, that I wasn't trying to rip 'em off. Plus, a lot of the bread I made on that first piece went to Mexico to pay my people's expenses and for more shipping.

When the first shipment came in, people started flocking to it, so it wasn't hard to sell. Lids are the most advantageous way to sell. If you were going to do it that way, you'd set yourself up in an apartment in San Francisco and sell lids for $15 or $20 apiece very easily. At least you could have then because there just wasn't any good weed around. Right now there's a lot of stuff around and everyone's holding onto it asking high prices, so nobody's buying. But when I got the first table, I could have sold it all as lids if I had wanted to sit on it long enough. If you're selling at $15 to $20 a lid, you're getting close to $500 a kilo, but that's the most risky way because you're dealing with more people and you have it around longer. So I sold a couple of keys here, ten pieces there, five pieces here, and so on. You sell it by weight, 10 pounds, 20 pounds, five pounds. You use an Ohaus triple-beam balance with a dial-a-gram on it so that it'll weigh within a tenth of a gram accuracy up to five kilos or so. It's accurate enough that if you want to measure hash to as close as a gram, you can do that, or if you want to sell weed in pounds and kilos, you can do that.

The price in the U.S. doesn't vary as much as it used to because young kids are hip to transportation. I know a couple of 19-year-olds who went directly from high school graduation to Afghanistan and scored 100 pounds of hash and brought it back, just like "Psssh!" nothing. I knew a guy 18 years old who was scoring from the guy in the Mexican prison I told you about. He was bringing it across the border to a house at the corner of Haight and Ashbury and selling it. He was shooting smack, all fucked up, but he'd been in the scene long enough already that he know the heat so well it was second nature to avoid them. He finally kicked smack a couple of years later, after his wife was gone, his friends were gone, everything was all screwed up in his life, but he was still managing to avoid the heat.

So anyway, I was offing pieces from the first shipment and waiting for the other shipments. They were supposed to be sending a unit once a week, but like I said, it took over a month for the first one to show up. Apparently what happened down there is that all my people went on paranoid trips about who was trying to rip off who, plus all the other insane personal shit going on, and I mean *insane*.

Goofy Gus got on a trip about Sally. I get this phone call from her one day after I'm back in the Bay Area and she is totally freaked out. She says, "Mika, you gotta get me out of here today! Gus threatened me!" She goes into this whole trip about how Gus threatened her life, she's locking herself in her room, all this heavy shit. Turns out it seems to be true. Sally has moved in with Domingo and Tanya and won't leave them because she thinks George is on Gus's side, and Gus is going completely nuts and wants to kill her because he wants to go to bed with her and she won't. Plus I'm gone with all Gus's papers and his car, so he can't go anywhere, he's got hair down to his shoulders and he's in a straight Mexican town with no visa, no birth certificate, no car, no money and no chick. He can't even leave the house, can't even go to a cathouse to ease his frustration. Since there's nobody else available he starts digging Sally because she's pretty. But he's no lady's man by any stretch of the imagination so she says no, and he threatens her. So she wants me to get her out of there right now.

I've got no money, right? I'm still waiting for the first table and I've already scraped together a couple of hundred and sent it to Mexico right after I got back into the States. All of a sudden Sally's screaming that I've got to get her a plane ticket. To do it I would have to sell my enlarger, which involves going into the city and more hassles and expense, just an incredible drain. Meanwhile I get a call from the guy Gus is working for saying that Gus has called him and everything Sally is telling me is a lie, and further that he has talked with George and George verifies Gus's side. So on one hand I have Domingo, Tanya and Sally telling me Sally's version is true and on the other hand I have Gus and George telling me it's a lie. I really don't believe any of them because they've been down there in isolation for so long that they now have their own versions of reality, their own little worlds. The actual outside world hasn't existed for them for a month and a half. Gus's boss is trying to tell me his behavior is just a case of a child trying to act grown up. What kind of trip does he think chasing Sally around with a knife is? Sounds like severe juvenile delinquency to me. By now none of the people down there can handle each other, but no one will cop to it. I keep saying, "Look, if you need me to come down and help straighten things out, or help with something, I'll do it. If you want to get out of there because you're freaking out, I'll come down and help get the situation calmed down. You can get out or take a break or whatever you need to do." But Tanya is determined to show me that her trip with Domingo is what she's supposed to be doing, so she's going to stay there no matter what. Her talks with me are getting colder and colder, for no good reason as far as I can see except that she's trying to prove something to me. And I'm getting colder and colder toward her, too — as you'd expect under the circumstances.

I'm sure a lot of things were happening down there that I was unaware of. Plus there are other things happening to me up here. Like with Sally. She called me after she finally got back north and I was supposed to go see her, but I haven't been able to. First it was that first shipment coming in and racing around offing that first and trying to take care of business. And then I just suddenly happened to find a new lady I dig very much, so I'm not really interested in seeing Sally. I mean, I'd like to see her but I know it's going to be a real bad scene. She's real bitter. She got down there and got into more — and less — than she bargained for. It was unwise for me to bring her down there and get her involved in that trip, it's my fault that she was there and got stuck there. *Why* it was my fault and *why* I was unable to do anything about what happened are completely different matters. But she's really bitter even now. I'll have to go see her soon.

As long as I was down there, the petty jealousies and hassles never really got out of hand because I could keep an eye on everything and I could explain what needed to be done. After I left and the shipment went slow nobody there knew what to do to speed it up. Then people started getting really uptight. They were boxed in. It got so freaky that finally I couldn't even give them any direction from up here because I'd get one story from one person and another story from someone else, and I wouldn't know for sure how to respond to either one of them. By that time I was so tired of the whole trip that I just decided there was no way anyone was ever going to get me down there again as anything other than a tourist.

Oh, I considered going back a lot of times. I'd think there was no other way to straighten those people out and get that weed up here. But then something else would happen and they'd call and want more bread. I'd get pissed off because I would have already sent money and they would have spent it all and not really done anything. I have a pretty good idea who's behind all that kind of action, right? Domingo. So I think, "Oh, shit no, man! I don't want to go back to that trip." I mean, you'd have to be crazy, right? By this time Tanya's running as fast as she can toward Domingo, trying to make herself believe that's where she really wants to be. He's on a big ego trip about that, so nobody's getting any work done, everybody's too busy watching everybody else and being paranoid and greedy. To the point where they're sitting down there *starving*! I mean seriously. At several points, they had *no* money. And everybody up here who's been sending them money is finished because they've made promises and made promises and made promises and haven't come through on any of them. The first unit got hung up in Mexico City. They were supposed to send another one right away that didn't get here till three months after the first shipment got here. Three months is a *long* time when people are waiting — unheard of, man! We'd already been in Mexico five months so that's eight months to get two units up. They were just sitting on it while it rotted because they were being greedy.

See we were supposed to split it a certain way that we'd all agreed on it. We were going to move three units, pay all the expenses and bills that were owed, then split the rest of the pieces. But they've gotten so greedy they want to cut out everybody else and make everybody pay even more for what they're still sitting on, ignoring the fact that the investors already own it. Nobody's going to front them any more money because they haven't even shipped up enough to pay expenses. I'm not going to send them two grand to ship me a unit that I already own and neither is anyone else. They sit around down there and spend the money until they're broke and then ask for more, then spend all that, then do a little work, then be broke again and ask for more money, then do a little more, and three months later they're ready to send up the second shipment. I finally told them I wasn't sending any more money till I had some evidence that they were going to carry out their part of the business.

Meanwhile I started setting up other ways of getting the stuff up here. Because while all this is going on, I'm getting phone calls and being hassled and trying to get enough bread to investors to keep them happy and reassure them that they're going to get their money. The guy I got the bread from that came from The Outfit is getting real uptight. The people in Chicago are getting real heavy with

172

him so he says "You better get that thing done pretty soon or these people are going to come see me. I have my wife and my baby here, so if they come to see me I'm going to have to bring them to see you." I understand his position but I didn't know where that money came from when I got it, I thought it was his. I didn't hear about the Chicago gangster link till a long time after I got the money. I'd already spent it before I knew where it came from. Plus they were holding me responsible for an amount I never got. So I said, "You can do that if you can find me, but telling me they're going to come just means I'm going to make it hard. I want to pay my bills, I want to pay all that off, but I'm damned if I'm going to get killed. So just fucking catch me, man!" After I got back up here he started calling me at my friends' place, which was pretty uncool because they didn't have anything to do with the trip, they were just old friends who let me stay there until I got straight because they could see I was really screwed up the night I got there. This guy started calling every day and getting more and more threatening, and meanwhile, this table is not coming through.

I'm going through all kinds of changes behind it thinking "Wow! The Chicago gangsters are after me, the heavies, the bad cats!" I'm really bummed out about it and one day I start talking to a friend about it and he says, "Well, what are you afraid of? Are these guys really that heavy?" See, I've got Al Capone in mind when I talk about guys from Chicago. Darrell says, "Hey, you're pretty heavy, too." I go "Oh. Hmmm." So I start to think about it. I've been shot at, I've been beat up, I've had to shoot my way out of situations, I ripped off the mountain Mexican Federales! Then I think "Okay, let those motherfuckers come out here. Me and my friends are just as bad as him and his friends — at least!" And I stop really being concerned about that. Then he called and said "Okay, they're going to come out." I just said "Hey! Every other day you want me to call you and every time I call all you do is threaten me. If you're going to get it on, man, then get it on! Tell 'em to quit talking about coming and do it. They're full of shit. Send those motherfuckers out here!" I told him I was doing all I could. "As soon as I have that shit, you get paid and not before then. Your harassing me isn't going to make it happen any faster. I'm not ripping you off and you know it! Besides, you got a cat there in Mexico sitting on the rest of the shit. I'm only getting 30 or 40 pieces this load and he's down there sitting on another 640, so what are you talking about, me ripping you off! Shit!"

From then on, they cooled off a lot. They really had me scared for a while. But who are those cats? A man is a man. Some are stronger than others and some are faster and some are better with a gun, and some are better with a knife and some don't care about any of that shit, they'd rather just live in peace. But if you stir somebody up bad enough, it doesn't make a bit of difference how big the threat is or how bad it's supposed to be, if you stir up anyone enough he'll rip doors off their hinges. I've seen it! You know how big my brother is, he only weighs about 120 or 130, and I've seen him tear places apart, I've seen him grab hold of a closed door where the pin of the latch is inside the door casing and just literally rip the thing right out of the wood! And he was only in high school then. Fear can do it, too. Fear can drive a guy to the point of blind courage. All of a sudden he just says "Let me out of this corner!" and anyone or anything in front of him better be strong or he'll tear them up. I'm like that, too. It takes me a long time to rise to that pitch, but once I get there, I don't give a shit about anything. When anybody starts that threatening shit, there's only one way to respond. So that doesn't bother me any more. I'll worry about it when it happens, and if it happens I'll take care of it as best I can.

Anyway, the people in Mexico are supposed to keep

sending the shipments and I'm supposed to keep sending expense money and we're supposed to keep it going like that till all the pieces are shipped. What actually happens is that I get the first shipment and sell the pieccs and send two grand down plus various amounts of other money over several months. Each time I send money, they're supposed to do their part. Each time there's a delay and nothing gets done. I don't really know what happened down there, I have so many versions of what happened after I sent money down that it's impossible to choose one. All the scenarios are fairly likely and fairly possible and maybe all of them are true some way or other, but the shipments that were supposed to follow the first one didn't happen. Finally, I arranged for other people to go down and pick up various portions. I hassled with it as long as I could then I was just finished. I couldn't hassle with it any more. So then we considered and used several different methods of getting parts of the stuff across the border.

The cat tied into the Chicago money went down first, but took the longest to get back. The helicopter airlift happened in the meantime. See, when I got the first shipment, I sent the Chicago cat a big chunk of that bread, then arranged for them to go down with some people they had who were capable of picking up more. They got part of their part back up and moved a part for me, but they still don't have all their share across, some of those pieces are still stashed down there somewhere. I don't know if they plan to go back and get them, that's all their trip now. The last time I talked with them they weren't interested in going back down given the scene in Queretaro, it was so insane. But they're paid off now as far as I'm concerned, they're cool, they're taken care of.

My brother brought about a hundred keys across a missile range down around Yuma, Arizona, walked it across the mountains, about a 35-mile hike. He and a couple of other people drove it as close as they could get to the other side, then loaded it into three backpacks and hiked at night into an area they knew was military — but they didn't know it was a missile range. They were supposed to meet another guy with a truck at the north end of the military reservation, then drive it up to Phoenix but they lost the map with their route. My brother stashed it so nobody would see it beforehand, but stashed it so well they couldn't find it when it came time to go. So they went out there blind, at night, and they got lost with no food and very little water and walked around in these mountains for two days with the stuff on their backs, until they found the missile range and started looking for the truck they were supposed to meet. Planes were flying overhead and 12-foot-long missiles were buried in the sand and they had no way of knowing if or when one of those things was going to come out of the sky. The cat who was supposed to meet them had been there and looked for them for a long time, couldn't find them and left, and then came back again. They just by chance happened to bump into each other! Then the four of them got lost again for another day driving around the missile range trying to find the way out. They finally did make it. So a hundred keys came across that way.

Another hundred came across in the false bed of some kind of big truck. Another 300 pieces came across by driving it up near the border and having a helicopter pick it up off the back of the moving truck, and fly it across the border to a prearranged location. The chopper pilot you met here the other night when we were talking will tell you that story, You can call him Captain Trueheart, he'll dig that because let me tell you, he is really a far-out cat! He's flown oil explorations and pipeline expeditions to the Grand Canyon. Chicks fall dead over him. I mean he's a really handsome, dashing cat. When he's flying, makes no difference what it is, if he thinks it's possible then it doesn't even have to be probable. If somebody says "Can you carry this pipe over the edge of the Grand Canyon, slack 4,000 feet, fly over a bridge and under some wires and then back down and go forward and swing the load onto a dock at the bottom of the canyon?" he thinks it over a bit and says, "Oh, yeah, I think so. Yeah, I can do that." And he jumps in the ship and does it.

I flew with him over the edge of the Grand Canyon and he did that to me — on purpose, of course — just sort of nudged the ship up to the edge and dropped it so it fell about 3,000 feet POW! just like that and then pancakes and pulls it up and — aw, shit, man, have you ever fallen 3,000 feet? I got into the thing thinking we were just going to take one of those nice, slow helicopter descents and all of a sudden I'm strained up against the underside of my seatbelt and I'm thinking "Something's very wrong, man, something's not going right!" Captain Trueheart's pretty far out. He's unbelievably lucky. He's crashed two or three helicopters, crashed into a granite cliff face one time and lived. He didn't really want to talk to you about our trip because he doesn't know you, so he did a couple of tapes with me about his trip to pick up our weed. Here they are. They'll tell you all about it.

Chapter 18
Captain Trueheart's Tapes

A brief history first, I guess. I met Mika in the mid-'60s, somewhere around in there. I'd known his brother for a while and we ran into each other going back and forth between Arizona and California a lot. We had talked about a year and a half ago of trying to coordinate a job coming out of Mexico with a helicopter. So this past October when I got through with a gig somewhere else I stopped back in Phoenix on my way to the coast and saw Mika and Samuel. It was the first time I'd seen them in more than a year. Mika looked real bad. The last time I'd seen him looked like about 180 or 190, but when I saw him again in Phoenix, if he weighed 130 that was really squeaking it out.

In the course of that conversation about what everybody had been doing, they ran down this story about what had happened in Mexico. We thought right from then on that we ought to try to get a helicopter and pull some of that weed out of Mexico. There were a lot of loose ends so we left it in October that I would look for a ship and once I located one, we would figure out a plan. I'll try to keep this as much to the point as I can, but it's really hard because a lot happened. It's hard to remember all the where, when and so forth. It was always just "If we can get it together." That's the way it went the whole time and we really didn't know till right at the end that it was going to be for real. So let's lay out the plan first, the way it was supposed to go, and then I'll tell the way it actually went.

First I'll throw in a short rundown on the helicopter industry. It's not solvent except for a few companies that have a lot of ships that they can fly year-round. But there are one-, two- and three-ship operators who think they'll just jump in and make a quick buck. This is good in summertime if you have a ship that's paid for or leased, but in the winter it slows down because the only place you can do any flying is in fair-weather country: California, Arizona, someplace like that. There really isn't a lot of construction or anything else going on in winter for helicopters. So almost every winter this leaves some poor guy with a helicopter he's got about half paid for and he's starving because he can't get any work for it. So when I got to the coast I made various calls trying to locate somebody sitting around starving to death. It didn't take very long till I found a fellow who was hurting pretty bad.

We made an arrangement for a guaranteed fee — and he really made out on that — plus he charges $100 a day for the ship. He's a straight cat, he doesn't know what it's going to be doing, all he knows is he's getting a lot of bread for not asking questions and he thinks it's going to be used for photographic work. He knows we need it for a certain amount of time. We agreed to rent for three days minimum to a week. Plus his guarantee. We didn't tell him I was the pilot, he never even saw me, I had a friend pick the ship up. The owner didn't know anything about me and I didn't know anything about him except what I had picked up through the grapevine.

Then it was a matter of talking with Mika to find out when he could get his people together and get the thing rolling. When that happened, it really got into serious planning. I got aerial maps and road maps of the area. The aerials are an especially good thing, they shoot a picture and the map comes right off the picture, so it's really accurate and concise. I originally planned to meet a vehicle on the road where this stuff was in Mexico to bring it up. I would pick it up on Route 2 and take it over to Interstate 80 and drop it onto another vehicle there. But that got to be too big a hassle because of the communications and other things, it was just too much, so we eliminated the vehicle north of the border. We came up with, I would pick it up from the vehicle in Mexico and take it to a farm south of Los Angeles where the people were cool.

So then I went down to the area where we were going to do the pickup. I covered all the roads on both sides of the border by car and found a place in the mountain range between San Diego and Yuma with lots of service roads. I found a place for a fuel stash because this would be a fairly long trip. I stashed 30 gallons of fuel in six five-gallon jugs beside a service road. The ship I was using didn't use much fuel, probably 15 or 16 gallons an hour, and I went down there with two full tanks, which is about 57 gallons on this particular ship.

I spent quite a bit of time in the Mexicali area just covering all the roads I could find to see what they looked like and find out where some of the check points were. But I was a little concerned about the things I didn't know about them, like how many people were stationed at each one and how many were narcs, and on this side, where the California Highway Patrol would be, just overall how many police there might be to contend with. I was a little worried about that, thought about it a little bit, you might say.

A week before all this was supposed to start for real I was down in the area again, just trying to find out who was where and who was doing what as far as local gendarmes and I ran into a kid who knew the whole scene. He knew exactly who was where and when and even knew the cats by name! He had it right down. So then I knew where people were who might throw up any resistance and figured out a route around them.

The only real hangup we ran into was getting a VHF transceiver to the people where the stash was in Mexico, because we discovered that for the actual pickup, trying to communicate by telephone just wasn't going to get it, there were too many loopholes, it was ridiculous. So we managed to get a VHF transceiver for the truck that would be coming up Route 2. The helicopter already had a VHF radio, and a transceiver is an all-channels transmitter and receiver that can be mounted in a car and run off the car's power. We got one and sent it down with instructions on how to use the cargo hook that would be dangling down under the helicopter. One fellow would have to ride in the truck with the driver and hook this thing up. It's pretty hard to find somebody in Mexico who's done it. I was just hoping the cat would have presence of mind enough not to get hung up in it or something like that.

The way it was supposed to go was the driver would start from the stash in Queretaro and go as far as Hermosillo. Someone would give us a phone call just to let us know he was on schedule, and then a little farther on, in Sonoita, he would let us know he was within three hours of the place where I was supposed to pick it up. When he called from Sonoita I would pick up the ship in San Diego and run across to the pickup spot. I was going to fly from San Diego across the pass down to this Laguna Salada area where the pickup was going to be because it was a big open space. We were doing it just before Christmas with a full moon so we could see pretty well at night. I would pick it up right off the moving truck so he didn't have to stop and it would be all bagged up in a big net weighing like 600, 650 pounds. He would drive there, we'd be in as constant radio contact as possible, I'd pick it up and go back across the border super low into the mountains. By then, it would be daylight and I'd hit the fuel stash and refuel and fly to the farm.

I decided, because I'd had enough experience to know it's the best way to do heavy loads, to use what's called a sling load. The cargo is put into a sling that's attached to a cargo hook under the helicopter. It was an advantage to us because the helicopter would already be in the air when the load was picked up, so you don't have to break ground with a big heavy load. It's much easier. Once you're in the air with it, you can pickle it, I mean get rid of the load from inside the helicopter, there's a button with a release on the hook. You can jettison the whole thing if you have to — a circumstance we were considering, you might dig. If the stuff is *in* the helicopter, you can't get rid of it, you're just stuck with it. So it was a way out if it came to that. In the truck we'd have the two people, one driving and one in the back to hook up the sling load, so it could be done very quickly. I had never done that, which was kind of neat, and I would be doing the refueling by myself. With a sling load it would be easier to land for that and take off again alone.

I picked up the ship and took it to San Diego to begin with. When the stuff got to Hermosillo I would move it to a place in the Mexicali area still on the American side but closer to the pickup area. Then I'd wait for the driver's phone call from Sonoita. When he got to San Luis he would call again and that's when it would really start to get heavy because then it would be less than an hour to pickup time. So the whole thing had to be real together from Hermosillo on. We were going to try to get the pickup to where it could be done at about 4 in the morning, when it's just starting to get light. That has a lot of advantages. You can see in the mountains, and its a real drag to fly through the mountains when it's dark. Also, at that time of morning everything is fairly quiet, people aren't doing too much. People are sleeping or just getting up and not really out and about paying attention to what's going on.

We wanted to get this done December 24th because the moon was coming on. It was cold, the moon was in Gemini, a good sign for transporting something, it's a good time of year. The important part was getting the truck into Hermosillo by 4 in the afternoon because that was 12 hours from where we were going to do the pickup and we wanted to do it and get into the mountains before daylight. One change was that I brought the helicopter to the stash point around the 23rd because I got to thinking that if it was in San Diego when the driver called from Hermosillo, then I'd have to make a night-time trip across the coastal mountains.

So okay, we were looking for the call from the driver from Hermosillo around 4 o'clock the afternoon of the 23rd, but that came and went and nothing happened. We thought, "Well, maybe we won't do it till Christmas Day and that'll be cool." We figured the driver probably had some trouble and couldn't keep the time schedule and decided to lay over for a day to keep the 4 o'clock timing going. Well, about 7 o'clock that night the phone rings and it's him and he says he's in Hermosillo and on his way. That means he's going to get to the pickup spot about 7 in the morning. I'm thinking, "Wait a minute, it can't be this fucked up, the original timing is the most important part of the whole plan." I'm thinking now it's going to be one of those daylight things, and that would be a big mistake. Then I thought, maybe not. Things like this happen, it's not out of the realm of possibility. But it brought a lot of pressure because we really didn't want to do it in broad daylight. Daylight at a later point in the operation would be cool because I'd be out of the area, but we needed darkness for the pickup and for coming across the border. So we hoped that maybe the driver would figure out that he's too late and cool it for a night. We had no direct contact at that point because the helicopter was stashed and the VHF transceiver in the truck wouldn't be on yet, so we could only hope he postponed it.

If he went ahead, it meant we should get a phone call from Sonoita around 1 in the morning. We waited and waited and 1 o'clock passed, and 2 a.m. came and went, so I figured "Great! He's figured this one out!" So we all turned in around 3 in the morning. Two hours later the phone rings and the cat is in San Luis, which is two hours from pickup! I like to went through the God-damned roof! I'm going up a tree because by the time he was going to be at the pickup area it would be daylight. We should have done the pickup an hour ago and the dude is still two hours away! I was all set to say "Well, just fuck it, because we're going to get nailed on this one." Then I got to thinking. The driver didn't have any instructions what to do and I can't just tell him to stay in San Luis on the border with 300 kilos. So then we figured what the fuck, it's gone this far, might as well go ahead. So we decided, "Okay, come on ahead!" I was blowing my mind, just pacing and pacing, going in circles in my head because of this timing screwup. Then Fate sticks its fickle finger in.

For three or four days before this there'd been all this kind of like smog hanging over the whole area. You couldn't see anything, you had a visibility of maybe three miles. I thought of this around 5:30 and went out to take a look. It was starting to get light and sure enough, the gunk is still there, so at least we have that much going for us. So I'm at the helicopter still pacing around, it's set to go, the sling load is on and it's checked out, it's cool. I'm so nervous there's no way I can eat breakfast. Twenty minutes from the pickup time, I'm in the air, I start off across the tules, 10 feet from the ground maybe, as fast as I can go, this is it. I've got all kinds of things running through my mind. I crossed Interstate 80, everything was cool, flew around the end of Calexico/Mexicali, went over Route 2 in Mexico and and headed for the spot. When I cross Route 2, I try to raise these guys on the radio, but I'm not getting any answer. This starts to really freak me out because the radio in the truck is a pretty good unit, you can hear it anyplace. I knew it worked before we sent it down there so I'm thinking something got screwed up, and now the pucker factor is really up there, it's *terrible*! I get where we're supposed to hook up and nobody's there, so I radio them again and this time they picked it up. Man! They said they were almost there so I said I'd be there to meet them. I start along this road and pretty soon I see this vehicle coming. Sure enough, it's them. I radio that I've got them in sight and then it's just a matter of getting the stuff out of the truck.

This guy climbs out of the cab of the truck and all I can see is he's back there doing something. As I get closer I see he's undoing the tarp and it's starting to billow and billow and billow and finally it just flies off onto the side of the road. By this time I'm coming up behind them and the guy is standing in the truck with the hook in his hand. It looks good, just the way I told him to have it, so I come up behind them and park her low trying to judge what speed they're at. The last time I looked at my airspeed indicator before I got over them I was doing about 45. Hovering over a truck at 45 isn't too hard, but I hadn't ever done anything like that before, so I came up over the back of the truck and just lined up the skids with the front fenders of the truck. Getting it down close enough to the truck so the guy there can get it hooked up was a different story. It was a while before I knew I was in the right position because I couldn't see the guy under me. He forgot to bring the radio microphone out with him so we can't talk. It probably would have been too much for him to handle anyway, but I get to where I can feel him pulling on the bottom of the ship so I know he's got hold of it. Then I feel two strong tugs, so I know it's hooked up. I start to pick it up off the truck and I feel it hit the line so I know from there on it's just a matter of lifting it out of the bed.

I pull and pull and pull and pretty soon I get the funny feeling that something isn't quite right, that somebody miscalculated how much 300 kilos is, because I know the load is off the bed of the truck but it isn't coming up. So finally I just pulled it all up and thought maybe it was just a figment of my imagination. But it wasn't. The side rack of the truck had gotten hung up on the net and I had been trying to pick up the whole side of the truck until finally the rack or the net gave away. As I pull away from the truck I can see it going down the road, but now it's only got one side rack.

So now it's time for me to beat a hasty retreat. I

head back over the end of the lake. Just after I did that, I looked at the shadow of the helicopter with this 300 kilos of grass slung underneath it, and it didn't have the rack hanging off it, so I figured I was cool. I had a lot on my mind between there and Interstate 80. I skimmed across Highway 2 just over the top of the road, and by the time I could see Interstate 80 I knew I was out of Mexico and no problems yet. I hit the Interstate and from there to the mountains felt like the longest distance I'd ever covered in my life. I just couldn't get those mountains to come to me fast enough. The only thing I saw between there and the mountains was a crop duster going along at about the same altitude as I was, but in the opposite direction. He just wiggled his wings a little bit. For some reason it struck me funny and I started laughing.

I got into the first set of hills and and the next step was to find the road to the fuel stash. I knew where it was but it seemed like I'd never get there because seconds were taking minutes and so forth and all this time I had to stay real low to keep out of the radar. Once I got into the mountains it was just a case of following the ridges because they can't pick you up that close. So I find the road, I go screaming up along it following all the curves. It didn't seem it should take so long, but I knew by certain landmarks that I still had farther to go. I'm flying along and it suddenly just went right by underneath me, I never even saw it. I saw the space so I circled around to come back, set the sling-load down, backed the ship up, set her down and I guess I was still running on adrenaline because I left the engine running and you never saw anyone leave a helicopter so fast in your life.

The stash was down an embankment off the road and I remember as I was struggling up the hill with two full jerry cans I was thinking "Jesus! You sure hid it good enough, you didn't stop to think how much of a hurry you were going to be in when you got here." Took two jugs at a time, three trips getting the stuff up there, pouring it in the tanks, throwing the cans inside the helicopter when I was done and then taking off again. When I took off I noticed how much the weather had changed. When I was flying low it was all this smoggy stuff but as soon as I got into the mountains it cleared. When I took off from refueling it was just really pretty because it was a clear day up there and there were two blankets of junk, one on one side and one on the other down close to the ground. So for a while I was just flying along thinking of other things, not conscious of what I was actually doing.

By this time I'd been able to pick up more altitude and I noticed that as with a lot of sling loads that have funny shapes — because it was square and the wind would catch the corners of the square — I noticed it was swinging back and forth, back and forth under the helicopter, like a clock pendulum. Most times, that's annoying because you can't do anything to correct it, but this time it wasn't annoying because it reminded me of other sling loads I've had on like it so it just seemed normal. It took my mind off what was in there because by now it was just me alone with all this weed. I thought some about why was I doing this, then I'd think a little more and every time I'd realize what I was doing, I'd just kind of grin. And of course you'd have all these thoughts and second thoughts running through your mind because it's just not something you'd do every day of the week. But I was much more relaxed after that gas stop and it was getting to be a lot of fun. Over the ranges of mountains, just tracking the roads down to the farm. There were other aircraft flying by, and every once in a while I'd turn to look and make sure they didn't turn around and come back. But nothing unusual happened between there and the farm, really, other than I felt a little conspicuous. That was only because I knew what was in the sling. Nobody else would even have any reason to think about it because there were other helicopters working in that area, people wouldn't think anything about it.

Coming into the farm was a trip. The people there knew I was coming and pretty much when since I would be able to adhere more to a time schedule in the ship than in a truck so we all knew within 15 minutes when I'd be there, given the good weather. They have a pasture behind the house, I knew where it was, I didn't have any trouble finding it, but I was sweating it all the time up there worrying about whether I was actually in the right place. I do that when I navigate, I get really uptight. As I started getting into the area where the farm is it finally hit me that it was almost done. Of course, it flashed through my mind, what if the gendarmes were sitting down there waiting, what then? I get the place in sight and shortly after that the people inside heard me coming. They came out of the house like, well, shit! Probably something like Kansas City did after the Super Bowl, like raving maniacs, just jumping up and down and the whole thing. When I got close enough to see the smiles on their faces it hit me: it was cool, we'd done it! I was grinning so hard it was all I could do to get the thing set down. I got out and we just jumped up and down for a while — it was really something, it was far out!

After that it was just a matter of taking the ship back, paying off the dude, no problem there, he was none the wiser, he was just really happy to get the bread and we were really happy to use the ship. We paid him and that was about it for my part of the trip.

Chapter 19
1970: Mika's Wrap-up

So there's been a fantastic amount of delay, the people in Mexico all got on a trip, they're still on it, and ended up at each other's throats. They ended up with this huge pile of weed. As long as I was there I could keep them all sort of cool because I just really cut myself loose from emotion, I cut myself loose from those chicks and all that. I didn't care what anybody's personal feelings were as long as I could keep them cool enough to keep the trip together. So I was running around playing Scotch tape. After I left there was nobody to fill that function because they were all stoned out on their own emotional trips.

What finally cracked it was when they sent that second unit up. There'd been a three-month lag between it and the first one and we'd already gone ahead and arranged other transportation for a lot of the stuff. Tanya's being real salty with me on the phone, it's getting colder and colder between her and me. But finally they were supposed to be sending up another unit and what happened was, they almost got us all busted. I go down to the shipping docks and as far as I know, I'm the only one who knows these units are coming, so I'm making arrangements to pick them up and how to disperse them and all that. The day I go there, somebody else is there at the same time to pick it up because Tanya has promised it to two people and given both of us the information on how to get it. How she got these other parties involved, I don't know. I got at least three different versions of that story, each one in one way or another contradicting the others. Yet the last time we'd talked she says she can't understand why I don't believe her!

I do know that apparently what happened was that after I'd already sent money down there, she got other money from somebody else. And she promised this unit to both of us and let both of us know it was coming without either of us knowing the other knew about it. Which is really a bad thing to do because then there are two parties checking with the Customs people, checking with the freight people, and so on. If the Customs people had any brains at all, which fortunately they didn't seem to have, they would have put it together that something was weird about this shipment.

Anyway, I get to the freight docks to pick it up and there's another guy looking to pick it up. We get into a big hassle right outside the freight terminal. I knew the cat, but I didn't expect to see him there to pick up the same unit I was picking up. I knew *somebody* was coming because I'd called the freight terminal to see if it was in and they said yeah, it was in and that Mr. and Mrs. So-and-so were on their way to pick it up. We were posing as a decorating company, so I knew something was amiss. So I called back the freight company and told them there'd been some confusion in our office, that shipment wasn't for *that* couple, it was for someone else. Then I went down to head them off and we got into this big hassle.

I could see that the cat had some bread, so I offered to give him part of the shipment to make up for the money he'd sent down there. He got real salty and started threatening me and giving me a bunch of shit, so I said, "Okay, go ahead on, you know you ain't going to get it." He went in with this xeroxed copy of the shipping bill that Tanya had sent him and they looked at it and said no, there'd been some mistake, it wasn't that shipment, so he got nervous and couldn't do anything but split. I had the actual shipping invoice copy so I went in and got it. But all of us could have gotten busted right there.

I talked to Tanya on the phone one night when you were over here taping and just told her to forget it, I wasn't sending any more money, I wasn't paying them to send any more of the weed up here because of what had happened.

She told me she didn't send the other guy the papers, and I told her that not only did he tell me she sent the papers, I saw them, so she must have sent them because he had no other way to get them. She'd also told him she sent three pieces instead of two and I just said "Somebody's lying and I don't know who it is and I don't really care at this point. You can have the rest of it."

She said, "Look I'm not trying to burn you."

I said, "As far as I'm concerned, you already have."

Then we went through this long conversation about the split and how that was supposed to have gone down, and what it ended up was, she wanted me to send her another four grand and then she would send the rest. I just said, "Hey! No! You know, just *no!*"

She says "Well, that's the only way you're ever going to get any more of that merchandise." I said, "If that's the way you want to leave it, groovy."

So then she gave me some shot about somebody else who wanted to come down and get it, but she didn't want to just screw me out of it, but she wanted to handle it on her own terms. I said "Hey, you know, if you have somebody else interested, then go ahead on because I'm past caring about that weed, I'm doing a lot of other things and you can have it." So that's how we left that.

If she gets reasonable, which it seems like she might do based on this other thing she has set up with this other cat, then it might go down and it might not, but if it does, that will take care of all that. Unless they decide they want to ship the rest of it on the original basis we agreed to, they can keep it. I don't care. I'm past hassling. I've been hassled with it as long as I possibly could. I've been hassling with it since May 29 and that's — what? almost a year now, a whole fucking 10 months anyway. Up until that last phone call it's been pretty much a steady basis, every waking hour of every waking day of every week of every month during that time. I've had it. I've had it with jive,

I've had it with seventeen different people telling me seventeen different reasons why something's not getting done and everybody promising it will get done for sure tomorrow and then that not happening. And people saying they're going to do things and they're going to keep their mouths shut and it's going to come soon, and then fucking it up at the last minute by opening their trap to somebody else who has no business being in it, at that point especially. I'm tired of sticking my neck out when I don't even think that's what's happening. Tired of danger coming from some direction I have no way of anticipating because of having confidence in various people at various points that was just misplaced. I don't have confidence in any of these people any more, they're all jiving me in one direction or another, and I have no way of figuring it out without just spending *all* my time figuring it out.

I'm doing other things now. I want to play my guitar and train my dogs, I'm not going to miss that stuff anymore.

I mean they've been down there so long that they have some isolation sickness of the brain, they really do. They're deceiving themselves. They think they've got something they don't have. They think they're sitting on a pot of gold, but one day it's gold and the next day it's mold, that's where it's really at. I keep trying to tell them that they're just going to sit down there and be paranoid and greedy and screw around and end up with nothing. That's where it's at now because nobody's going to go near that stuff, everybody has already heard and been through the changes. Anybody who might possibly call about that weed isn't going to be interested in the way they're trying to do it because they're just screwing everybody around. Tanya's giving me this stuff about going other places with it and I'm saying "Okay, go. Do whatever you want to do. But consider me out."

Because the only way I can do anything about it

would be to go back down there and hassle with them. I don't need it. Why at this point in my life would I want to do that? I can just sit here and talk to you and do a much better thing for myself than go back down there. Knives and guns and all that shit? I don't need that. If I want to get in a knife fight I can just go downtown and do it, I don't have to buy an airplane ticket to Mexico City.

The rest of the grass is sold and everybody's got their part of the bread out of it, so that part of it is pretty much wrapped. The people who had to be paid off are paid off. For me it was a loser, I don't think I even made expenses this year. And as far as I'm concerned, I'm pretty much out of it. I got other things to do, other ways to spend my time. Got this pretty, black-haired girl to run around with, got this book project that we're getting into. I should spend my time worrying about those fucking idiots? No way!

So I'm getting out of it.

Well, that's sort of true. I still … I don't know. Like these people out of my past have problems and when they call up and say they're in trouble, they need money, you hate to let an old friend down. I keep telling them I'm not sending any more money, but then I always end up sending it. But I'm going to have to quit this business, you know. At some point I'm just really going to have to quit and just … you know. I think I've got it all worked out now so that somebody's going to go down there and take care of all that shit and get everybody out of there, so then that'll be finished.

You know what it is, is *hook*, man! It's adrenaline. Adrenaline is probably addictive and by putting yourself into certain situations you can really make your body produce a lot of adrenaline. And every time, it's really a flash! You know, until you just finally completely flash yourself out, I guess. You just keep pushing the button to get that electricity again. It's like, what you do for adventure. That's certainly got to be part of people's impulse when they do something like weed smuggling. I mean, maybe you do it once as a fool, going down into Mexico to score weed, and you want to make a lot of money and everything like that, so you go down there and find out what the trip is like and how close at hand death is and all that, but if you go back after that, you're a thrill-seeker.

Or maybe it's just that you have some kind of weird devotion. It gets to be a craft, you get to be good at it. It's like talking to people who are carpenters, who don't know how to do anything but be carpenters or furniture makers or something like that. You get into it so heavy that when you turn around and start to get out of it, you find that it's a long, gradual process of separating yourself from something you've been living with for years.

But I think I'll get out of it. I've been a warrior long enough, I'm tired of battling. That's where I'm at. And things are too pretty in my life right now to go hassle in Mexico anymore.

A Postscript

Shortly before pushing the "publish" button on this book, an article by Amanda Chicago Lewis in the March 9, 2018 edition of Rolling Stone magazine alerted the author to yet another aspect of marijuana use: the dangers of chemicals used by growers and the fact that, for example, California still did not have regulations to oversee this aspect of the plant's growth and uses. Other publications including the Washington Post, have also covered this facet of the herb's emergence as a legal substance, whether for medical or recreational use. The reader is advised to pursue this topic further on the Web. But to sum it up briefly, as Lewis put it in her report, "If you like pot you have absolutely exposed yourself to chemicals that can damage your central nervous system, mess with your hormones and give you cancer." A word to the wise.

– **Robert Loomis, 04-23-2018**

Comm Restitution
$9^{30} - 1 1^{30} A$
$130 - 5$
$6^{30} - 9$

76193236R00111

Made in the USA
San Bernardino, CA
09 May 2018